Competition in a Dual Economy

Competition in a Dual Economy

JOSEPH BOWRING

PRINCETON UNIVERSITY PRESS

PRINCETON, NEW JERSEY

Published by Princeton University Press,
41 William Street, Princeton, New Jersey 08540
In the United Kingdom:
Princeton University Press, Guildford, Surrey

Library of Congress Cataloging in Publication Data will be
found on the last printed page of this book
ISBN 0-691-04234-9

Publication of this book has been aided by a grant from the
Whitney Darrow Fund of Princeton University Press

This book has been composed in Linotron Sabon

Clothbound editions of Princeton University Press books
are printed on acid-free paper, and binding materials
are chosen for strength and durability
Printed in the United States of America
by Princeton University Press
Princeton, New Jersey

Contents

List of Tables

Acknowledgment

I am grateful to those who established and continue to maintain the unique graduate program in economics at the University of Massachusetts at Amherst; the faculty and graduate students with whom I studied there could have been assembled at no other institution in this country. I would like to thank Richard Edwards for providing encouragement and intellectual stimulation during the formative stages of this project as well as criticisms and ideas that resulted from his subsequent readings of the manuscript. I would also like to thank for their invaluable help Robert Averitt, Ron Boheim, Jean Fisher, Bradley Gale, David Gordon, James Kindahl, Bruce Laurie, Ed Mathis, Don Michak, Michele Naples, Muffy Siegel, Al Woodward, and an anonymous reader for Princeton University Press. I am of course solely responsible for the contents of the book. A summer research grant from Villanova University facilitated the process of making revisions to the empirical analysis.

Philadelphia, 1985

Competition in a Dual Economy

CHAPTER ONE

Firms, Industries, and Competition

THE theory presented in this study is in the broad tradition of economic analysis, which has attempted to come to terms with the role and significance of the very large corporation in our economy. This tradition includes the neoclassical models of oligopoly and monopoly; models of imperfect competition and oligopoly behavior; models of workable competition, limit pricing, and contestable markets; Marxist models of monopoly; managerial models of the large corporation; Galbraith's related theory of the "planning sector"; and dual economy analyses.[1] What ties this tradition together from the perspective of the present study is a common concern with how, if at all, the rise of large corporations has affected the way in which competition takes place and thus economic performance at the firm, industry, or macroeconomic level. Each of these theories or models is at least in part a theory of competition. They each address the question (if sometimes only implicitly): How do large firms compete and how do the systematic results of that competition compare with the results under atomistic competition where there are assumed to be no significant, persistent heterogeneities in the universe of firms? This tradition may be characterized generally as suggesting that insofar as the existence of large firms has any effect on competition, competition is reduced by their presence.[2] Further, industries dominated by

[1] For example, Robinson 1933; Chamberlin 1933; Baran and Sweezy 1966; Sweezy 1942; Sosnick 1958; Sylos-Labini 1969; Marris 1964; Galbraith 1967; Averitt 1968.

[2] There are certainly exceptions to this generalization (including Joseph Schumpeter) but the consensus interpretation is that the presence of large firms reduces competition. Other analysts suggest that size by itself is not enough. For more on this question, see, especially, chapters three and four.

large corporations are thought to be unusual for that reason and to represent more or less isolated islands of oligopoly in the stream of competition.

This broad tradition of analysis can be usefully separated into three strands, each of which encompasses a substantial amount of diversity: the formal neoclassical models of oligopoly and monopoly; the industrial organization tradition which attempts to address the institutional realities of competition from the neoclassical perspective; and the dual economy approach which suggests that firms and/or industries can be grouped into two broad categories for analyzing competition.

The present study attempts to define the dual economy approach more precisely than it has been to date, to formulate a derivative set of testable hypotheses, and to subject them to empirical testing. While it is within the dual economy tradition, the theory presented here will be termed the core–periphery theory. Throughout the book the core–periphery theory is contrasted primarily with the industrial organization tradition, which is defined more precisely in chapter four, and both core–periphery and industrial organization analyses are contrasted with the neoclassical model of competition.

The theory of core and periphery is consistent with and builds upon both developments in the study of industrial dualism, the dual economy tradition, and developments within the field of industrial organization. Though initial developments in the analysis of dualism focussed on firms and industries,[3] the principal focus of recent interest has been the derivative structure of labor markets, termed labor market segmentation.[4] Common to empirical studies of industrial and labor market dualism has been the conception of the industry as the unit of analysis. That is, it is assumed that the most important differences separating the two principal sectors of the U.S. economy are based on industry characteristics.

[3] Steindl 1952; Galbraith 1967; Averitt 1968; O'Connor 1973.
[4] For example, Gordon, Edwards, and Reich 1982; Edwards, Reich, and Gordon 1975; Cain 1976.

Some authors writing from the dualism perspective have suggested that the sectoral distinction should focus on individual firms.[5] This position is consistent with the core–periphery argument made here that there are important distinctions between firms in a single industry and that the heterogeneous internal structure of industries makes them inappropriately aggregated for analyses of firm performance. There may, for example, be firms with periphery characteristics in industries which are classified as core industries because they are dominated by core firms. This second, firm-specific part of the dualism literature has not previously been subjected to empirical testing for broad sectors of the economy. In the case of the labor market segmentation literature this is principally a result of the lack of labor market data at the firm level.

The core–periphery analysis also builds on the relatively new development within the field of industrial organization of a more sophisticated approach to the study of industry structure and performance. The literature of strategic groups suggests that industries are too complex structurally to usefully study as units and that more detailed examination reveals that there exist within industries clusters of firms with common attributes, termed strategic groups.[6]

These attributes derive in part from the different strategies chosen by firms as a means to the common goal of profit maximization. The attributes which may distinguish strategic groups within an industry include: the nature of production technology; the degree of product differentiation, vertical integration, and diversification; and the nature of formal organization and control systems.

These important distinctions between groups of firms within industries are also associated with differences in performance. Again, the important conclusion of this literature is that a focus on industry characteristics alone is not an ade-

[5] Averitt 1968; Steindl 1952; Sweezy 1942.
[6] Critical works in this literature are Caves and Porter 1977; Porter 1976; Newman 1978.

quate guide either theoretically or empirically to an analysis of
the performance of firms in an industry.

This book will focus on the firm-based theory of dualism,
which is consistent with the convergence of these developments in the study of industrial structure on the importance of
intraindustry, interfirm distinctions. However, while the core–
periphery theory draws on these elements of the tradition of
analysis identified above, it breaks with various aspects of that
tradition in several important respects.

Within the industrial organization literature the usual view
of interfirm competition and the industrial structure accords
the firm and the industry equal importance in the analysis.
This approach views industries as composed of firms which are
qualitatively identical although they may vary along any of
several dimensions, principally size or output; the firm is
uniquely a member of its industry and is in a sense defined by
its industry membership. Higher firm profits, in this view, are
associated with efficiency or a lower position on the industry
cost curve. Group dynamics like collusion may or may not
play an additional role within particular industries. In this
sense the industry is the unit of analysis while firms give the industry internal structure and provide the mechanism for working out the imperatives of industry technology mediated by the
individual characteristics of the firms.

The theory of core and periphery takes the firm as the unit
of analysis. This implies that, while industry location is important and some aspects of firms' market power can only be
defined relative to an industry, there are significant firm attributes which are independent of particular industry membership. In the theory of core and periphery, salient firm attributes
serve to organize firms into two large groups regardless of specific industry membership. Rather than being essentially undifferentiated, firms can be classified into two broad, qualitatively different groups, core and periphery on the basis of
differences in size and joint market share, which in turn imply
differences in competitive behavior, performance, and market
power.

Core firms, which exist as the result of an historical process that has proceeded over the last century, are thus defined to be large relative to all firms in the economy, and to possess significant joint market share in one or more industries, which together result in market power. Periphery firms are all those which do not meet the twin criteria for core membership. Thus, large firms without significant market power and small firms with and without market power are all members of the periphery. Within the simple two-group classification, there may be firms in transition from core to periphery and from periphery to core. Large firms without significant market share may be in this transitional group, as may be profitable, rapidly growing small firms, but in both cases such firms are included by default in the periphery category. Some such firms may ultimately join the core group. Large firms with significant market share in shrinking markets may also be in this transition group although they are currently included by definition in the core group.

Core and periphery firms by this definition frequently coexist within individual industries; and within industries, as in the economy as a whole, core and periphery firms constitute groups with distinct patterns of behavior and performance. Periphery firms are not necessarily "mom and pop" operations nor are they necessarily family-dominated entrepreneurial-style firms. Many periphery firms are relatively large in the universe of all corporations and many have traditional managerial corporate structures. Thus the core–periphery distinction is not equivalent to either the large–small distinction or the owner–managerial control distinction.

Within the industrial organization tradition, firms with significant market power represent isolated outposts noteworthy for that reason, but they have no direct part in the formation of the normal rate of return which results from a generalized competitive process among the majority of firms. Interindustry capital flows are not systematically treated in the industrial organization approach. The majority of industries do not represent outposts of oligopoly power. Competition serves to regulate the profit rates of all firms across all such industries, it is assumed, but details of a plausible institutional mechanism to accomplish that regulation on a sufficient scale are left unspecified. For oligopoly-dominated industries it is frequently assumed that potential entry constitutes a limit on firm profit rates, although the model provides no general explanation of the sources of the new investment, actual or potential.

In the core–periphery view, while core firms are not individually isolated, the competitive dynamic which involves core firms is itself isolated from the competitive dynamic among periphery firms. Thus, rather than small groups of noncompeting firms surrounded by a generalized process of competition, the core–periphery hypothesis is that there are two generalized competitive processes or regimes, one in which only core firms participate and one in which predominantly periphery firms participate.

Further, it is hypothesized that these two distinct competitive regimes have characteristics quite different than those imputed, explicitly or implicitly, in the traditional view. The hypothesis is that active core firm competition, particularly on an interindustry basis, results in the formation of a relatively homogeneous group profit rate when compared with periphery firm competition, which is hypothesized to be largely intraindustry and which produces only a weak tendency toward the formation of a group profit rate; there is a stronger tendency toward an equal rate of profit within the core than within the periphery.

Core firms tend not to engage in active price competition within their home industries. Rather, they adopt a form of behavior which recognizes the mutual interdependence of their pricing decisions, termed corespective behavior, which is consistent with maintaining relatively high profits among the core group in an industry. Core firm investments in new industries, or diversification, provide a profitable outlet for the reinvestment of earnings not always available in the home industry, and create significant interindustry capital flows. It is hypothesized that these capital flows and the associated direct and potential competition between core firms, frequently with different home industries, contribute to the formation of a core rate of profit.

The competitive regime of core firms is inaccessible to routine access by periphery firms as a result principally of size-related barriers to entry. It is argued that core firms' investments contribute to their market power within individual industries by raising new entry barriers as well as by contributing directly to profitability. Periphery firms, limited by lower profits, are generally isolated in single industries and in the periphery sectors of single industries and tend not to engage in interindustry competition. As a result, periphery firm profit rates tend to be more heterogeneous than core firm profit rates.

Thus the core–periphery hypothesis is that periphery firms tend to be isolated in individual industries by a combination of exit and entry barriers, while it is core firms that engage in more active interindustry competition. Such competition, however, does not carry with it the normative connotations of neoclassical competition; there is no presumption that society receives the benefits of core firm competition. In the core–periphery model there is a bifurcated process of competition which results in the formation of two distinct rates of profit rather than a single normal rate of return, which is the usual outcome.

The size, joint market share, and resultant market power of core firms, together with the absence of active price competition among core firms within individual industries means that the outcome of the core firm competitive process is quite different from that among periphery firms. It is hypothesized that a principal result of the dual competitive process is that core firms earn profit rates that are systematically and significantly higher on average than those of the periphery group.

Further, it is hypothesized that the market power of core firms allows them to earn not only higher profit rates than periphery firms but also profit rates which are significantly less risky than those earned by periphery firms. The profit-maximizing strategies of core firms simultaneously produce profits that are higher and less risky than those of periphery firms. The structural advantages of core firms, which permit higher profits, also provide lower risk. The hypothesis is that the bifurcated competitive process produces two distinct relationships between risk and return; while there is an intragroup tradeoff between risk and return for both core and periphery firms, core firms enjoy superior performance on both risk and return measures when compared to periphery firms.

This study defines the core–periphery theory more precisely than previous efforts to address industrial dualism. In addition, this study examines in detail the industrial organization literature, which is where much relevant theoretical and empirical work appears, for consistency with the core–periphery theory. Finally, a set of independent empirical tests of the theory are performed on a data set constructed for this purpose.

Chapter two presents the theory of core and periphery as a theory of competition and develops the theory in terms of firm goals, the structure of industries, and interindustry capital flows. The chapter also presents a set of derivative, empirically testable hypotheses. Chapter three reviews historical evidence on the evolution of the industrial structure, patterns of diversification, trends in aggregate and industrial concentration, and the stability in the ranks of very large firms, and demonstrates the general consistency of this evidence with the theory of core and periphery.

Chapter four reviews other perspectives on competition, principally those embodied in the literature of industrial organization and in the somewhat more scanty dual economy literature. Chapter five reviews the empirical industrial organization literature in areas relevant to this study. Results on profitability and size; profitability and concentration; more complex relations between profitability, absolute firm size, relative firm size, and industry concentration; and profitability and various measures of risk, are shown to be consistent with the empirical hypotheses generated by the core–periphery theory. Chapter six presents the empirical results from tests of the hypotheses of this study as well as details of the data set and empirical methodology.

CHAPTER TWO

Core and Periphery Competition

THE theory of core and periphery in the U.S. economy is a theory of competition. In order to survive, core firms have altered the form and nature of their competitive behavior several times since the late nineteenth century. Core firms are not pitiful, helpless giants fated to topple and rot into Marshallian senescence; their competitive adaptations have made them virtually indestructible. Their continued aggregate dominance of the economy is almost certain. From this perspective the industrial structure has been both cause and result of such strategic changes on the part of dynamic core firms; the interaction between the industrial structure and the behavior of core and periphery firms is a basic determinant of the performance of firms, the structure of profit rates, and the distribution of capital in the economy.

From the perspective of core and periphery, competition between core firms is currently the dominant form of interindustry competition in the U.S. economy. However such competition does not carry with it all the normative connotations of the competition of neoclassical theory; the fact that core firms compete does not imply that society benefits. On the contrary, the nature of core firm competition further isolates them from the eroding effects of competition from outside the core. While growth and technical change have permitted significant new entry into the core group in this century, such entry has served to extend and buttress the aggregate position of core firms. Active core firm competition is consistent with the ongoing core domination of the economy; core firm competition is consistent with a core rate of return significantly higher than that which prevails elsewhere in the economy.

The perfect competition of neoclassical economics is a useful benchmark for theories of competition; it provides the basic elements which must comprise any model of competition. Three such elements are the goals of the firm, the structure of individual industries, and the nature of interindustry capital flows. The neoclassical model requires that firms maximize profits, that there be a very large number of sellers in a market, and that there be perfect capital mobility. The result of the second condition is that no single firm can influence the price. Every firm takes the price as given and the industry profit rate is determined by the difference between that price and the costs of production. The result of the third condition is that profit-maximizing firms enter industries where above-average profits exist and leave industries where they earn below-average profits. When all firms are free to move across all industries, and the second condition holds, an equal rate of profit will prevail across the economy as a whole.[1]

While this formal model of competition does not reflect the institutional realities of the current industrial structure and the forms of competition which characterize it, the model is relevant as a benchmark and because it defines what a complete theory of competition must include. Firm goals, industry structure, and capital flows will be considered in the following analysis of how competition proceeds in an institutional framework characterized by core and periphery groups. (In chapter three, the way in which the formal neoclassical model of competition guides this study is distinguished from its role in the literature of industrial organization.)

GOALS OF THE FIRM

There has been some disagreement over the goals of large corporations within the tradition which has analyzed such firms. Short-run profit maximization, long-run profit maximization, sales growth maximization, managerial job, salary, and per-

[1] Bator 1957.

quisite protection, and the quiet life have been proposed, among others. Assertions about the dominance of various forms of nonmaximizing behavior derive in general from that part of the tradition which views large corporations with market power as less active competitors and which focusses on the industry itself as the primary locus of competition. Pursuit of the "quiet life"[2] or satisficing[3] assume that firms have market power sufficient to provide such isolation from competition, and that nonmaximizing behavior is an option consistent with long-run survival as a dominant firm. In the core–periphery view the competitive pressures on core firms within as well as outside of their principal industries mean that nonmaximizing behavior is not a plausible goal.

Various forms of maximizing behavior have also been proposed as consistent with large firms' observed performance. In the core–periphery view, active and potential competition between core firms both within and between industries implies that only profit maximization is consistent with growth and survival as a core firm. Pursuit of objectives other than profit maximization would mean the ultimate eclipse of the firm and its probable decline from core status via direct competition or valuation-inspired takeover. In the core–periphery view the position that other objectives are paramount overstates the degree of protection afforded by barriers to entry in a dynamic setting in which new technologies arise and industry boundaries themselves may shift.

Long-run profit maximization is equivalent to the goal of maximization of long-run asset size or the rate of growth of assets over time. If profits are reinvested in the firm (assuming a fixed dividend payout ratio), maximizing the present value of the stream of future profits is equivalent to maximizing the asset size of the firm at any point. There is no choice to be made between maximizing the growth of assets and maximizing long-run profits.

[2] Hicks 1935.
[3] Cyert and March 1963.

As the goal of long-run profit maximization is to be interpreted here, it does not necessarily entail the usual set of assumptions associated with the theory of short-run profit maximization. For instance, the goal of long-run profit maximization need not require perfect knowledge of either investment opportunities or the likely consequences of those investments. Here it is held to imply only that core firms attempt to maximize long-run profitability via any techniques available to them.

Long-run profit maximization is more plausible than short-run profit maximization for core firms because they are long-lived entities and are assumed to have their own persistence as an essential part of their objective function. Short-run profit maximization is not relevant to core firm behavior for several reasons. Short-run profit maximization in the neoclassical sense assumes a fixed capital stock, while core firms are here assumed to have a planning horizon which incorporates investment decisions as well as the associated expected profit streams. Further, short-run profit maximization can actually conflict with the long-run perspective of core firms and thus with profit maximization over time. For example, the price increases associated with a short-run profit maximizing strategy could encourage new entry and ultimately result in lower profits or failure.[4]

Periphery firms are also assumed to have profit maximization as their goal, but periphery firms have a much shorter time horizon than do core firms. The relatively safe assumption by core firms that they will ultimately reap the benefits of a long-term strategy is not correspondingly safe for periphery firms, which face predation by core as well as other periphery firms.

The debate about firm goals has its origins in Berle and Means's study, which suggested an evolving separation of ownership and control in large corporations.[5] Subsequent studies confirmed the original finding and demonstrated that

[4] See chapter four for elaboration.
[5] Berle and Means 1932.

the extent of the separation is still increasing.[6] This trend may result in a parallel divergence in firm goals if managers have different goals than owners. Managers, it is argued, may be more interested in the stability of the organization and in maintaining the associated perquisites of power and thus may tend to be more risk-averse than owners. Or, managers may be more interested in objectives like sales growth maximization than in profit maximization.[7]

The structure of management compensation is alleged to contribute to the divergence of goals between owners and managers. If management compensation is determined primarily by sales growth rather than the profit rate, managers could be expected to emphasize sales growth over profit maximization. Empirical tests which relate compensation to variables associated with alternative managerial goals produce somewhat ambiguous results. However, despite problems with the definition of compensation and with specification of the hypotheses, the results suggest that profitability is a major determinant of managerial compensation.[8]

The potential extent of managerial prerogatives in goal selection is constrained by a number of external factors. The threat of takeover is frequently cited, although the evidence suggests that apparent nonmaximization of profits plays a much less significant role in inducing takeovers than other factors, like firm size.[9] Profit performance is directly related to managerial power in that the reward of high profits includes high stock prices, superior credit ratings, and thus improved access to the external capital required for firm growth.[10] In more general terms the "competitive environment" constrains firms and managers from straying too far from profit maximi-

[6] Burch 1972; Herman 1981; Larner 1970.

[7] See, for example, Baumol 1967; Galbraith 1967; Marris 1964; Marris and Wood 1971; Penrose 1959.

[8] Herman 1981, pp. 85–113; Scherer 1980, pp. 35–37; Murphy 1985.

[9] Herman 1981, pp. 98–101; Marris 1964; Manne (1965); Singh 1971; Singh 1975.

[10] Herman 1981, pp. 98–100.

zation in that good profit performance is directly related to the probability of firm survival.[11]

Empirical tests of the relation between the form of control and firm performance show that owner-controlled firms earn higher profits than do manager-controlled firms but that the difference is very small.[12] Moreover, when market power is explicitly controlled for, the evidence seems to show no significant relation between profitability and control form by market power categories.[13]

The long-run profit maximization hypothesis can be logically distinguished from the long-run sales growth maximization hypothesis. The latter hypothesis as it has generally been presented implies a tradeoff between profitability and growth. However, the tradeoff derives from the restrictive assumption that the growth rate of sales is the sole target of the firm; this literature does not contest the positive association between profitability and the asset growth rate.[14]

Product sales can be stimulated by certain activities which incur costs and cut net profits. Marketing expenditures, advertising, and price cutting are all examples of such activities. Although these tactics may increase profits initially, after some point their cost in addition to the inefficiencies associated with rapid growth mean that as the growth rate of sales continues to rise the rate of profit will fall.[15]

It is certainly possible for growth by any measure to be too rapid and therefore destabilizing to the managerial structure of a firm, with the ultimate result a lower rate of profit. Rapid growth may result in organizational problems, inadequate planning, and under- or overinvestment in plant and equip-

---

[11] Scherer 1980, pp. 38–41; Jensen and Meckling 1976.
[12] See, for example, Elliot 1972; Larner 1970; Radice 1971. For a useful review of the statistical and conceptual problems with these studies see Herman 1981, pp. 106–112.
[13] Palmer 1973; Qualls 1976, pp. 89–104.
[14] See, for example, Baumol 1967; Marris 1964; Marris and Wood 1971.
[15] Marris 1964.

ment.[16] Such problems are likely to be associated with firms trying to maintain or establish market share in rapidly growing industries or with firms trying to establish a significant market share in industries they have just entered. In such cases there may be a short-run tradeoff between profitability and growth by any measure in the affected market.

The sales growth maximization hypothesis suggests that the tradeoff may exist in the long run for a firm if it chooses to maximize sales rather than profit growth because it may be possible to find a sustainable sales growth rate higher than that consistent with profit maximization. That is, the firm can move onto the downward sloping portion of the profit rate–sales growth rate curve and still earn enough profits to enable capacity growth to keep up.[17]

The fact that firms make expenditures on marketing does not itself create the tradeoff between profits and growth. These expenditures are clearly necessary for the most profitable reinvestment of capital. Firms plan investment and marketing strategies simultaneously. Given the goal of long-run profit maximization, the purpose of marketing expenditures is to earn the maximum profit rate on invested assets and thus to gain asset growth rather than to encourage the maximum sales growth rate. Investments in new capital stock are made according to profit-maximizing criteria. These investment strategies must consider product demand and thus marketing strategy and the costs associated with it. The existence of a tradeoff depends on the unlikely assertion that firms will choose to spend on marketing past the point where the return from such spending just equals cost. In other words, in order to make the tradeoff argument it is necessary to assume that a firm will overinvest capital in a market; a firm will invest capital past the point where it earns its maximum profit rate in order to allow increased sales growth rather than investing capital in new markets.[18]

[16] Penrose 1959.
[17] Marris 1964, pp. 234–60.
[18] Ibid.

While it is plausible, and consistent with the point of view of core and periphery, that managers pursue growth, it is not plausible that they pursue sales growth at the expense of profit or asset growth. Such a strategy would be ultimately self-defeating in that it would result in less than maximum growth of profits, investment, and in the long run, given a constant capital–output ratio, sales.

Even in theory, sales growth maximization and profit maximization are consistent objectives over a wide range of both variables. This reduces the likelihood that empirical tests will be able to distinguish the hypotheses. That likelihood is further reduced when it is observed that managers, whether pursuing their own goals or following owners' dictates, operate in an uncertain environment in which clear-cut choices between profit and sales growth maximization probably exist only infrequently.

The ambiguity of the empirical results in tests of hypotheses about the maximization of divergent firm goals is instructive. The measurable variation between the effects of such firm goals has been very small to nonexistent. It is consistent with the widely held view, and that of this study, that there is little if any operational difference between the various proposed firm maximands. In a dynamic and uncertain context the characteristics of firm maximizing goals are nearly indistinguishable in practice. These results are also consistent with the hypothesis that the principal goal of large firms is profit maximization, and that other plausible goals which have been suggested reduce, in practice, to profit maximization.

CORE FIRMS

The analysis of competition within industries dominated by large firms has also been the subject of some contention. A variety of formal models of large firm interactions in such industries have been developed and analyzed.[19] While a large part of

---

[19] For a review of this literature, see Scherer 1980, pp. 151–68.

this literature focusses on the behavior required even within an oligopolistic market structure to ensure joint profit maximization it has also been argued that noncompetitive behavior is not required in order for large firms to earn above-average rates of return; size alone is enough.[20]

In the core–periphery view, size alone is not enough to ensure above-average rates of profit. Explicitly collusive behavior is also not required. A combination of size and significant joint market share is enough to produce market power adequate to ensure consistently higher profit rates for core firms than for periphery firms. Further, it is hypothesized that the structure of competition within the core and the forms of that competition are closely related; in effect the forms of intracore competition produce important elements of the structure, which defines and delimits that competition.

At the opposite pole from the view that noncompetitive behavior is required in order to take advantage of an oligopolistic market structure is the view that large size alone is enough. It has been asserted that under certain conditions, the profit rate of large firms would exceed that of small firms in equilibrium even in the absence of noncompetitive behavior by large firms, as a result solely of the structure of competition. According to this argument, some investments cannot be attempted by any but very large firms because of the capital requirements associated with them. Large firm profitability is determined by the supply of capital in units large enough to undertake such investments relative to the potential for such investments. This implies, of course, that large units of capital are in effect a different factor of production than small units, and that capital markets are not perfect. In other words, small firms cannot in general assemble through accumulation or borrowing the amount of capital necessary to undertake large-scale investments.[21]

[20] This argument is made by Baumol 1967, chap. 5, and tested by Hall and Weiss 1967.

[21] See note 20.

According to this argument the competitive dynamic does occur but in two separate spheres with two separate results. The neoclassical model of competition assumes a supply of capital willing to invest in production in an industry as long as firms in that industry earn an above-normal rate of return. But, if the number of firms which can undertake large investments is limited, then full competition would result in an above-normal profit rate in industries which require such investments. Unrestrained competition between large firms would result in a higher rate of return than that earned by smaller firms elsewhere in the economy. In industries where no such capital requirement barriers exist, the larger supply of capital relative to investment opportunities would result in a normal rate of return.

This argument requires the assumption of full interindustry capital mobility because in the absence of such mobility, even under conditions of limited entry, intraindustry competition could drive large-firm profit rates down to the normal range or to the small-firm rate. For example, large firms in an industry might expand output and/or cut prices in an effort to increase market share and long-term profitability. With unconstrained interindustry capital mobility for large firms, the lower profit rates that result from intraindustry competition would exist only for a short period, as in the neoclassical model of competition. One or more large firms would shift to another industry accessible only to firms with adequate capital where they could again earn a higher rate of profit. Decreased supply in the original industry would allow prices and profit rates there to rise to the equilibrium rate for large firms. The same result would follow if long-run forces, for example, a secular decline in product demand, pushed the industry's large-firm rate of profit down. Thus, under the assumption of full capital mobility, the only conditions required for large firms to earn a systematically higher rate of return than all other firms is that the opportunities for uniquely large-scale investment exist, that such opportunities are available only to large firms, and that such opportunities are adequate relative to the supply of capital in large units.

There are two related problems from the core–periphery perspective with the hypothesis that large firms will, in equilibrium, earn higher rates of return than small firms. The assumption of full interindustry capital mobility and the assumption that there exist, as given by technology, investments that require large units of capital, are both problematic. The core-periphery hypothesis provides a consistent alternative view of a bifurcated profit rate formation process that requires neither assumption.

The assumption of full interindustry large-firm capital mobility is unlikely to be met in a world where investments are embodied in long-lived capital assets and where immediate liquidation and reinvestment are not real possibilities, particularly on a large scale. When this assumption is relaxed the simple existence of a surfeit of large-firm investment opportunities is no longer adequate by itself to explain the formation of an above-average large-firm profit rate. If firms cannot leave an industry when competitive pressures intensify, then the possibility of intraindustry competition between profit-maximizing firms means that large firms' profit rates could be limited to the normal level for significant periods of time. Without full capital mobility the advantages of size alone do not unambiguously imply significant long-term differences in firm rate of return by firm size.[22]

In the core–periphery view while core firm dominance does require capital investment beyond the reach of most firms, such dominance is part of an historical process of investment and competition which produces both a strong position for a core group in certain industries and a formidable set of entry barriers to those industries. Important characteristics of an industry which is dominated by one or more large firms are in large part created as part of the development of that domi-

---

[22] Steindl 1952 analyzes the macroeconomic effect of large-firm reinvestment problems.

nance rather than being "technical" characteristics inherent in the industry. From this perspective, capital is not highly mobile when the rate of return it earns depends heavily on the particular features of an industry. Thus the set of all investments accessible only to large firms is not equal from the viewpoint of a large, dominant firm in a particular industry. The advantages that core firms have built over time are not easily transferred to a new industry.

The result of the historical process for large firms in particular industries gives core firms substantial market power. Market power as used here means the ability of firms to affect market outcomes, particularly prices and profit rates, product attributes, and innovation.[23] The market power of core firms derives from a combination of large size relative to all firms in the economy and substantial joint market share. The requisite market share is not necessarily defined relative to a narrow market for a single good. In order to provide market power of the order of magnitude required for a core firm, the shared market or industry must have certain characteristics, principally large size and steady growth.[24]

---

[23] Shepherd 1982.

[24] Averitt 1968 and Chandler 1969 indirectly support this view in their analyses of core firms, "core industries," and the industrial incidence of core firms. Averitt defines a set of key industries; he argues that since manufacturing is essential to economic development, manufacturing industries are the most important in the economy. He proposes criteria for key industries within manufacturing that include: important forward and backward linkages, technological convergence, capital goods production, leading growth industries. The key industries tend, in his view, to be dominated by core firms.

In a detailed historical study of industrial concentration and large firm industrial location, Chandler argues that concentration occurred primarily in those industries that "are most critical to the strength, continued growth and defense of a modern, urban industrial and technologically advanced society." He reaches a conclusion similar to that of Averitt, that key industries have been and continue to be dominated by core firms. He uses Averitt's criteria to show that even in 1919 the top 100 firms operated in these key industries with only two exceptions.

Averitt and Chandler merely note these features of core firm location and use them to argue for the significance of core firms' place in the economy.

The development and maintenance of market power by large firms creates barriers to capital mobility. It creates barriers to entry into an industry by outside core firms and barriers to entry into the core segment by small firms from both within and outside the industry. The development of market power also creates barriers to exit.[25] Core firms have a strong reason not to leave their home industry; to do so would forfeit the accrued value of historical investments.

Size alone is not enough, substantial joint market share alone is not enough, and size and single-firm market share together are not enough to ensure core membership and the market power associated with that membership. Size alone is not enough in the absence of full capital mobility. Substantial joint or individual market share by other than large firms is not enough because if persistent above-normal profits are earned, large firm entry is likely; such a situation is expected to be relatively transitory. The combination of size and significant single-firm market share is also considered unlikely to result in stable market power. Such a situation can also be expected to attract large-firm entry or the development of a large competitor from within the industry if a single large firm with significant market share succeeds in earning persistent above-normal returns.

The domination of an industry by core firms has two salient features: it inhibits free entry by outside large firms and free

---

Clearly, core firms did not choose to locate in the most critical industries of the economy. The causality is a little more complex. These firms came to dominate those industries because those markets were large, stable, and growing and therefore susceptible to domination by a few huge firms. Industries that are critical in importance to the growth of the economy are almost by definition perfect locations for core firms because their important links to other industries imply that their markets can only expand as the economy grows and develops.

[25] Bain 1956 introduced the concept of barriers to entry. Caves and Porter 1976 analyze barriers to exit. Caves, Gale, and Porter 1977 have suggested that firm behavior can create barriers to entry both within and between industries. Caves and Porter 1977 extended the notion of entry barriers to include mobility barriers in general.

exit by core firms in an industry, and it entails significant intraindustry retaliatory power among core firms. This combination creates an incentive to avoid price competition for core firms.[26] Price competition by firms with significant market power means that such firms will earn less than the maximum profit rate available. If it is assumed that price cuts by core firms in an industry will be matched by other core firms with equivalent market power, then price competition is not a cost-effective method of competition for such firms. It will not result in a gain in market share, and thus will result in a decline in the profit rate.

All that the dominance of non-price competition requires is that core firms are assumed to recognize their own self-interest.[27] Neither the unrealistic behavioral assumptions of Cournot and those who followed his lead nor the explicit collusion assumption of George Stigler are required to explain the above-normal profit rates earned by such firms.[28] Non-price competition as the profit-maximizing strategy follows from the assumption by core firms that price cuts will be met by other core firms. Thus, any competitive advantage will be effectively nullified, in the context of exit barriers and limited capital mobility. There are a variety of complex factors which may limit the ability of core firms to maintain prices above the level that would produce normal returns. It is the core–periphery hypothesis, however, that on balance and via a variety of mechanisms, the interdependence of their pricing decisions outweighs any such limits.

[26] The argument of Caves and Porter 1976 that collusion may be less likely or less stable in the presence of exit barriers than in their absence depends on the assumption of a steeply sloped marginal cost curve in the normal range of operation. This assumption is unlikely to be met for core firms. See Scherer 1980, pp. 810–11.

[27] Scherer's summary statement (1980, p. 168), is instructive in this regard: "Any realistic theory of oligopoly must take as a point of departure the fact that when market concentration is high, the pricing decisions of sellers are interdependent, and the firms involved can scarcely avoid recognizing their mutual interdependence."

[28] Stigler 1968.

The "corespective behavior"[29] which results is an informal system of understanding based on the retaliatory power of the participants, on the related fact that profit maximization for each firm is linked to the behavior of all, and on the structure of market power. As the number of top firms in an industry increases, their absolute and relative size decreases and thus their retaliatory power can be expected to shrink and their structural advantages decline. Thus the return to active price competition decreases and the return to corespective behavior increases as the number of top firms declines. The result is that the profitability of the top firms in an industry may be expected to increase with their absolute size and their level of joint market share.

It is hypothesized that there exists some critical level of joint market share, above which large firms find corespective behavior to be the most profitable strategy, and above which corespective behavior results in increased profit rates for large firms. Above that level large firms have adequate market power to recognize and reap the benefits of corespective behavior; large firms as a result can earn profit rates higher than those resulting solely from large size. It is hypothesized that below that level of joint market share, large firms do not have adequate market power to recognize and reap the benefits of corespective behavior and do not have adequate market power to provide a level of profitability comparable to that of core firms.[30]

---

[29] The term 'corespective behavior' was introduced by Galbraith in *The New Industrial State* (1967). The term is broadened and extended here.

[30] No pretense is made here that this constitutes a fully developed theory of oligopoly behavior. The argument is that, given the structural conditions outlined in this chapter, core firms will find a way, or a variety of ways, to avoid the type of intraindustry competition that drives their profit rates to levels earned by other firms. No general assertions are made about the exact mechanisms that allow this result. Any or all of the great variety of such mechanisms preferred in the literature will suffice, from price leadership to explicit collusion. However, collusion is not required for successful core firm outcomes and is unlikely to be a typical means to that end. Corespective behavior carries no more general implication of explicitly or actively cooperative be-

The core–periphery hypothesis suggests that core firms have available a range of competitive tactics that are more cost-effective than price cutting and thus more consistent with profit-maximizing behavior. They include advertising, the creation of new consumer products via advertising, research and development expenditures and marketing initiatives, the creation of new capital goods designs via research and development, the expansion of the product line via internal development or acquisition, and the establishment of a service and/or distribution system. Such tactics should provide a residual or longer-term benefit because they cannot be matched either simply, immediately, or exactly, unlike price cuts.

Further, sequential rounds of such non-price competition do not require continuous decreases in price and thus profits. In the case of new products, for example, advertising costs represent a relatively constant proportion of product price for each product sold and do not require continuously increasing expenditures per unit and lower per unit margins, as with price cuts. Product differentiation tends to occur via a change in the type and quality of the advertising rather than an increase in intensity, although an increase in intensity may be associated with the introduction of a new product.

Of equal importance, it is hypothesized that non-price competition has a structural effect on industries dominated by core firms. Many forms of non-price competition while serving as a vehicle for intraindustry profit maximization, also result in the erection of barriers to entry, which further limit competition.[31] These forms of competition and resulting mobility barriers are part of the historical process that results in core-dominated industries. Investment in breadth of product line, diversification, vertical integration, research and development, advertising, and particular production technologies all contribute to barriers to entry to the core. While the barriers vary in specifics

---

havior. It is asserted only that aggressive intraindustry price competition will in general be avoided.

[31] This idea is also advanced by Caves and Porter 1977.

from industry to industry, they are a common feature associated with groups of core firms which dominate industries. These barriers serve to discourage entry by periphery firms both from within the industry and from outside as well as entry by outside core firms. Equally important, these barriers, established over time, discourage exit by core firms which could not easily reproduce them elsewhere. Core firms can also be expected to reap substantially greater advantage from such tactics than can periphery firms. For example, a core firm can spread the costs of national advertising over more units and therefore profit more from such expenditures than could a periphery firm in the same industry. Further, since core firms have large individual market shares, the benefits from advertising can be captured more reliably than is the case for periphery firms.[32]

The benefits of corespective behavior can be expected to accrue primarily to the dominant large firms.[33] Within an industry periphery firms with a vertical relationship to core firms are at a competitive disadvantage. They are not in a position to gain directly from core firm behavior. The benefits to periphery firms with a horizontal relationship to core firms are potentially larger but are limited by the types of competitive behavior that core firms do engage in. For example, product creation and differentiation, maintenance of a broad product line, and the creation of distribution and product service networks all serve to increase core firm profits but also to limit the associated benefits to a single firm, or at most the group of core firms.

In summary, the core–periphery hypothesis is that when large size and substantial joint market share are conjoined to produce market power, firms exist which are qualitatively different from all other firms. Core firms have the ability to make and to benefit from certain investments that are not available to smaller firms. The ultimate benefit that core firms derive

[32] Scherer 1980, p. 386.
[33] Caves and Porter 1977 also argue that members of "groups" within industries may exhibit significantly different performance.

from their investments is that the investments help to create further barriers to entry, while they contribute directly to higher profitability. These barriers to entry are also barriers to mobility, however. In order to earn profit rates above those earned by other firms, core firms must engage in corespective behavior. Core firms as a result of their market power are expected to earn profit rates significantly higher than those earned by periphery firms.

INDUSTRY STRUCTURE

In the core–periphery view, there are three general patterns of industry structure. In the first case most industry output is produced by a few core firms, while the remainder is produced by a small number of periphery firms. In the second case all or most industry output is produced by periphery firms and there is no core firm presence. In the third case there is a significant concentration of output in the hands of a few core firms, while the remainder is distributed among a substantial number of periphery firms.

The group of core firms in an industry will be termed the core sector and the group of periphery firms will be termed the periphery sector. Within each sector there may be segments, made up of one or more firms, that are significantly different from the other firms within the sector as a result of differences in the nature or breadth of the product line, the production process, invested capital, or pricing strategy. Such segments are more likely within the periphery sector than the core sector of an industry.[34] There may be intraindustry competition among core firms, between core firms and periphery firms, and among periphery firms.[35] The nature of intraindustry competition between core and periphery firms depends on the industry structure. In the case where there are only a few small firms,

[34] The concept of "groups" and "segments" within industries was introduced by Caves and Porter 1977.

[35] The following descriptions of intraindustry core–periphery competition draw heavily on Averitt 1968.

there are two primary types of core–periphery interaction. Periphery firms may be vertically related to core firms, either as suppliers of parts or raw materials on the back side or as retailers/wholesalers on the forward side. Periphery firms may also produce the same product as core firms; however, it is expected that they would typically produce only a subset of the full line of products, or specialized products without adequate volume to interest core firms. Thus periphery firms in such industries can be thought of as dominated by core firms. As suppliers or retailers, periphery firms are effectively price-takers because they have no significant leverage against core firms. As direct competitors in selected products, periphery firms must generally accept the prices and market share dictated by competition with the full-line producers. Periphery firms may also be affected more severely by cyclical fluctuations because they do not have other product lines to rely on and because core firms relegate periphery firms to more cyclically sensitive parts of the industry.

In the second type of industry structure, periphery firms compete only with one another. Where periphery firms survive as specialized producers or by a vertical relation to a core firm, competitive pressure on prices and profits derives primarily from core rather than periphery firms. In periphery-dominated industries, small firms compete without constraints from core firms within the industry. Periphery firms may compete to establish market dominance through price cutting, technological innovation, and marketing efforts. Entry tends to be relatively unobstructed in an absolute sense in such industries and new entrants may increase the competitive pressures. These forms of competition can be thought of as the regulators of the profit rates earned there.

In the third type of industry structure core firms, while still with significant market power, are faced with a much more substantial group of periphery firms. Such industries may be in historical transition. Despite core firms' advantages, several factors may allow the periphery firms to survive. The growth rate of industry demand may be high enough to accommodate expanding core firms along with many periphery firms, or the pricing policies of core firms may allow the periphery firms to earn a profit. However, as the internal growth rate of the core firms equals and surpasses that of the industry as a whole, they are likely to become more aggressive in attempting to sell their output. They may cut prices, or slow their rate of increase, and push marginal firms into losses and failure. They may also step up marketing efforts to increase their market share primarily at the expense of smaller firms which cannot afford to imitate them. As a result some periphery firms may be pushed out while some compete successfully with core firms to establish solid positions as periphery producers or sometimes even as new entrants to the core. It is hypothesized that in general this process eventually results in the first type of industry structure.[36]

INTERINDUSTRY CAPITAL FLOWS

Although they form a central part of the neoclassical analysis of competition, interindustry capital flows are generally ignored in traditional analyses of large firms and competition. Insofar as interindustry competition is treated in such analyses, it is generally assumed that such competition is least active among the large firms that dominate particular islands of oligopoly and most active among firms without substantial oligopoly positions.[37] By contrast, the core–periphery hypothesis is that interindustry capital mobility originates primarily with core firms and takes place via the process of diversification and subsequent intrafirm interindustry capital flows.

However, capital does not simply flow from one industry to another and large firms do not simply enter an industry with above-average profits. In the core–periphery view, large firms' choice among new investment areas is constrained by real institutional barriers, which range from a lack of specialized

---

[36] Steindl 1952 developed a model embodying a similar dynamic.

[37] For more on this point see chapter four.

knowledge or capability to the structure of the industry under consideration. Large dominant firms generally diversify into industries closely related to their basic industry along any of several important dimensions.[38] Similarities in distribution and marketing, in advertising techniques, or in production technology are, either separately or in combination, important links to a diversifying firm. These links allow such firms to bring to bear some or all of the advantages they have developed in their home industries. In the core–periphery view, diversification is the process of core firms extending their market power into new industries in a manner similar to that in which they established themselves originally and in which they maintain their current positions. Core firms use their access to large sums of capital, technological know-how, management skills, and the capacity for various forms of price and non-price competition to change the character of the industries they enter. Core firms create new "core industries" as they expand.

In contrast to the neoclassical model of competition and to the view embodied in traditional analyses of the large corporation, the core–periphery hypothesis is that the combination of capital mobility via diversification with the various structures of intraindustry competition implies a differentiated process of profit rate determination for the economy which does not produce a single rate of profit or simple equilibrium. At the same time, the results are not completely heterogeneous; two rates of profit emerge.

In the core–periphery view the direction of interindustry flows of capital is determined by the structure of competition within particular industries. The stimulus to capital flows lies both within the industries where such flows originate and in the industries to which such flows are directed. In contrast to the neoclassical analysis, however, in which capital flows generally originate in industries where firms earn normal or below-normal profits and are directed toward industries in which firms earn above-normal profits, in the core–periphery

---

[38] Berry 1975; Gort 1962; Rumelt 1974.

view these capital flows originate in industries where core firms systematically earn above-average returns and are directed toward industries where firms may earn on average the normal rate of return, below-normal returns, or above-normal returns.

Within industries dominated by them, core firms tend not to engage in aggressive price competition. Rather, competition constrained by barriers to exit and corespective behavior and protected by barriers to entry results in above-average core firm rates of profit. Within the group of core firms in any industry there are certain upper limits on profit rates earned there as well as pressures toward an equal rate of profit across core firms. Core firms' intraindustry profit rates are limited by both internal and external forces. The internal forces are a result of competitive pressures; marketing and other expenditures designed to maintain or expand market share limit firm profits, for example. In addition such firms face the external constraints that exist for any market, including the growth and elasticity of industry demand, technical and organizational limits on cost reduction, and potential entry from core firms in other industries. These internal and external constraints prevent profits from rising without limit while allowing substantially above-average profitability.

In core-dominated industries the argument is that core firms with approximate equality of resources and facing roughly the same set of internal and external constraints in the context of corespective behavior will tend to earn equal rates of return. In general it is assumed that no single firm has a systematic structural advantage which would allow it to earn significantly higher rates of return over a long period. It is of course the case in some industries dominated by large firms that one firm does have some systematic advantage which allows somewhat higher rates of return and that a technical or product-related breakthrough may provide such an advantage, at least temporarily. However, these do not represent the general case and competition should tend to reduce such advantages over time.

If core firms consistently earn high profits they face the

problem of where to reinvest them. Expansion of market share at the expense of periphery firms, periodic investments in new technology, and expenditures on marketing and research and development all provide an outlet for investible funds. However, these activities share the characteristic that while they may expand both firm and industry demand and thus postpone any active constraint on intraindustry growth, they all increase profits when successful. It is hypothesized that ultimately the growth of profits exceeds the capacity of the industry to absorb them at the prevailing rate of return, reinvestment in the industry earns a decreasing marginal profit rate as the marginal effectiveness of marketing expenditures declines, and the rate of growth of production exceeds demand growth for the core firms.[39]

The core–periphery argument is that a mature production technology and a saturated market mean finally that core firms earn more than they can profitably reinvest in their own industry. Core firms are driven by their success to invest outside their own industry; they continue to reinvest in their own industry only until the profit rates there are comparable to what they can earn elsewhere. It is this dynamic which is hypothesized to create important interindustry flows of capital. It is essential to add that in the core–periphery view the proposed dynamic is a complex one that does not imply a simple choice between investing in the home industry or diversifying. Core firms will simultaneously invest in a range of subindustries with different characteristics within the home industry, and in one or more new industries.[40] Core firms in such a situation face a continuum of investment options. The maximum marginal profit rate may shift between new industries and the range of occupied subindustries. The hypothesis nonetheless is that ongoing domination of the home industry creates pressures for new investments outside that industry. Diversification thus serves both to extend the market power of core firms

[39] See Steindl 1952 for a similar argument.
[40] Clifton 1975 makes a similar argument.

and to relieve the pressures for more intense competition within the home industry which might threaten their market power even there.

It is hypothesized that core firm entry into new industries can take two forms: entering other core-dominated industries or entering industries populated primarily by periphery firms. Core firms face problems similar to reinvestment in their own industry when they attempt to enter other core-dominated industries. The establishment of a profitable market position by entry into such an industry requires a large investment and entails a significant risk of failure because success can come only at the expense of an already dominant firm. The risk is presumably heightened by the existing firms' experience in the industry; core firms' dominant position results from an historical process that is difficult to duplicate by entry over a short time.

The potential for core firm entry into core-dominated industries does exist and constrains, via some form of limit pricing, short-run profit maximization by core firms in their home industries.[41] Given the risks associated with such entry, this potential is only likely to be realized under conditions such as persistent above core-average profit rates in combination with demand growth rapid enough to make postentry profitability seem attractive.[42] The hypothesis is that the real threat of potential entry and the pricing and investment strategies designed to forestall that threat provide one mechanism that operates to establish an equal rate of return among all core firms, across industries. Barriers to all but large-firm entry and large-firm market power limit the pool of potential entrants and tend to assure both that the core firm profit rate will not be forced below the core average by new entry but also that it cannot rise dramatically above that earned by core firms elsewhere.

As a result of difficulties associated with invading other core

[41] See also chapter four on limit pricing.

[42] Given that profitability is the real magnet, not the level of prices per se, Caves and Porter's (1977) characterization of this as "limit profit rate" may be apt. For an analysis of the determinants of such an entry decision see, for example, Sylos-Labini 1969.

firms' primary territory, the argument here is that core firms will tend to diversify into less tightly structured industries or to build new industries via product differentiation and/or the creation of new products. Entry into such industries can take place through building of production facilities, establishment of distribution and procurement systems, and intensive advertising, or by the route of acquiring a company in the industry. In fact, because periphery firms as a group are highly heterogeneous, large firms often have the option of acquiring very profitable leading firms within industries of small firms. In one move they can acquire a leading position within an industry and a profitable firm, which can then be expanded with all the capital, technology, and experience of the core firm.

The profit rate earned on investment in new industries is limited by expenditures associated with expanding as well as production costs, demand conditions, and the intensity of competition. After an initial entry phase, the profit rate earned in the new industry or industries becomes the limit for the overall firm profit rate. This marginal profit rate is the maximum marginal profit rate that the firm can earn. If the firm could earn more in its home industry it would do so.

The core–periphery view of this aspect of the process of profit-rate formation within the core is, then, that regardless of their initial industry profit rates, as core firms invest in new industries the profit rates earned there will begin to affect overall firm profit rates. That is, the average profit rate for the firm will tend to approach the marginal profit rate, whether the marginal rate is higher or lower.[43] New areas with good profit potential will attract entry by more than one core firm and frequently these core firms will have different home industries. Individual core firms may enter more than one new industry at the same time or over time.

This direct competition to enter profitable "periphery industries" will create a tendency toward equal marginal profit rates

[43] Sweezy 1942 details a similar dynamic but reaches very different conclusions. See chapter four for more on Sweezy's analysis. See also Clemens 1951.

across all these core firms. If firms in a particular new industry earn above core-average profits after some core entry, further core entry will be encouraged or, if the marginal profit rate earned by a core firm after entry is below core average, the firm may simply leave the industry and try another one. As the process itself expands, the firms gain new expertise and the process is reinforced. Successfully diversifying firms are likely to continue to diversify and to do so into areas less and less directly related to their original industry.

The hypothesized result is that the overall profit rates for core firms will tend toward equality. Their equal marginal profit rates will force their average profit rates toward equality, even if they are unequal to begin with. The hypothesis is that capital mobility by diversification contributes to the tendency for profit rates to be equal across all core firms.

The outcome of the historical process of core firm diversification is the existence of large firms with market power in a range of subindustries. It is proposed here that such firms will shift resources between subindustries in response to their varying profitability, and as a result the profit rates earned in each subindustry will tend toward equality. This process should also contribute to an equal interindustry intracore rate of return, insofar as core firms with different home industries face one another in some subindustries. In a sense, diversification is just an extreme form of this behavior. Large diversified firms shift capital between a variety of subindustries in response to profit differentials and in some cases shift capital into new industries as relative profitability dictates.

This broad process, which includes actual entry via diversification into both core-dominated industries and periphery industries but primarily the latter, and the threat of potential entry into both categories of industry, creates a tendency toward an equal intracore rate of profit. This process is limited by various technical and organizational barriers. The hypothesis is not that every core firm could successfully enter any industry, nor that every core firm would attempt to do so; but since there are common areas of competence and expertise among core firms, direct competition will take place and potential competition will represent a credible threat.[44]

PERIPHERY FIRMS

The core–periphery hypothesis is that core firms will tend to earn systematically higher rates of return than do periphery firms as the result of a set of advantages, summarized as large absolute size and substantial joint market share, which are reproduced through the forms of core firm competition. The correlate is that periphery firms will tend to earn lower rates of return on average than core firms. Price and product competition among periphery firms within industries contributes to this lower return as do intraindustry and interindustry interactions between periphery firms and core firms. In addition, periphery firms in general do not have significant market power and they do not have the resources to compete in all the ways favored by core firms.

For core firms a relatively homogeneous profit rate is the result of lower limits on profitability derived largely from shared market power, the associated corespective behavior, and diversification, and upper limits on profitability derived largely from actual and potential competition both within and between industries. In the core–periphery hypothesis, no comparable pressures exist for periphery firms. The competitive dynamic for periphery firms produces a relatively wide dispersion of profit rates.

In the core–periphery view, there is little active interindustry periphery competition because periphery firms are generally confined by limited resources to their home industries. For periphery firms, competition is largely intraindustry, either with other periphery firms or with core firms, but even such intraindustry interaction is not as significant for periphery as for core firms in equalizing group profit rates.

Active intraindustry periphery competition of a type consis-

[44] Rumelt 1974.

tent with the neoclassical model of perfect competition would result in reduced intraindustry periphery firm profit rate dispersion. Such competition would require that periphery firms be able to shift to a new industry if profits were not adequate, that periphery firms be relatively homogeneous, and that high profit rates among periphery firms in an industry would attract new entry. However, the conditions required for such competition, free exit, free mobility within periphery sectors and free entry, do not exist in adequate form to reduce the profit rate dispersion of periphery firms to a level consistent with that of core firms. Given that these conditions do not exist, the core–periphery hypothesis is that active competition within industries among periphery firms will result in a relatively wide dispersion of profit rates across the entire periphery group.

The only lower limit on periphery firm profitability is provided by failure and/or exit. It is hypothesized that for periphery firms, as for core firms, exit is not free or costless; investment is industry-specific and the salvage market for the capital equipment of unprofitable firms is restricted. In addition, periphery firm mobility is more like that of the perfectly competitive model, in which the entire investment in an industry is liquidated and reinvested elsewhere, than core firm mobility, in which only marginal investments are shifted to new industries. The result is that the lower limit to periphery firm profit rates is below that which would obtain under conditions of free exit. While the actual lower limit for core firm profit rates is also provided by failure and/or exit, the generally effective floor for core firm profit rates is provided by a combination of market power and corespective behavior. Thus the effective lower bound on profit rates is hypothesized to be significantly lower in relation to the group mean profit rate for periphery firms than for core firms.

Mobility barriers are not a problem faced solely by core firms contemplating entry into another core-dominated industry or by periphery firms attempting to gain entry to the core. Periphery firms face a complex set of industry-specific and/or segment-specific mobility barriers that inhibit free capital mobility within and between industries and thus inhibit competition.[45] The nature of success and failure for periphery firms is somewhat idiosyncratic; there is substantial interfirm variation within the periphery sector in a typical industry. It may be difficult for a periphery firm to mimic successful firms if success requires substantial new investment. There may be segments within the periphery sector of an industry which consist of several firms producing the same product under the same or similar conditions. Entry into such segments may be difficult for existing periphery firms again if it requires substantial new investment.

Mobility within the periphery sector of an industry is also limited because those periphery firms which would most benefit from mobility, those with below-average profits, are least able to change strategies within an industry or shift to a new industry. They do not have access to sufficient resources. In addition, those firms with relatively high profit rates are not likely to earn such profits consistently over time.

These are not barriers which would in general have a serious effect on the investment decisions of core firms, yet they may have such effects for periphery firms. The significance of mobility barriers varies with the type and size of potential entrants; the relative height of mobility barriers is critical. Barriers that affect the intra- and interindustry mobility of periphery firms may be much lower than barriers required to inhibit core firm capital mobility.

Periphery firms are more likely to take advantage of small market niches that offer the potential for high but temporally unstable profit rates. Thus because periphery firms tend to be short-run profit maximizers and because competition for periphery firms is somewhat unsystematic, a periphery firm may, at a particular time, have profit rates comparable to or higher than those of some core firms.

Intraindustry as well as interindustry mobility barriers may

[45] Caves and Porter 1977 introduced the general notion of mobility barriers in the context of segments within an industry.

be more significant for periphery than for core firms. Core firms' retaliatory power is premised on the ability of any core firm within an industry to compete directly and effectively with the other core firms across the full range of industry products. This is the basis for corespective behavior, which results in the relative homogeneity of core firm profit rates within an industry. This ability, based on the rough equality of core firms and their large resources, does not exist for periphery firms. Limited periphery firm resources restrict mobility and potential or actual competition within industries with significant product heterogeneities.

The hypothesis is not that these intraindustry mobility barriers create permanent high-profit enclaves for some periphery firms, nor that they are insurmountable. Despite imperfect mobility, intraindustry periphery firm competition does serve to limit the profit rates earned by periphery firms on average as well as the maximum profit rates which successful periphery firms can earn. The hypothesis is that periphery firms have significant heterogeneities; that these heterogeneities limit the extent of intraindustry competition; and that the result is significant variation in intraindustry periphery firm profit rates.

Active interindustry periphery competition would result in reduced profit rate dispersion. Periphery firms can, like core firms, enter either core-dominated industries or industries populated primarily by other periphery firms. However, neither is part of a systematic process of interindustry capital mobility by small firms. As a result of generally low and temporally unstable rates of return, periphery firms do not have in general adequate resources to engage in diversification and they do not face internal pressures for such investment similar to those which face core firms. Again, those periphery firms with the greatest incentive to change industries, those with below-average profit rates, are least able to do so.

Another potential source of effective interindustry competition for periphery firms is capital-market financed new entry. If new firms enter industries with above periphery average profit rates, interindustry intraperiphery profit rate differentials should decline. However, the same mobility barriers will affect such entry as affect intraperiphery mobility. They will have a similar effect on the dispersion of profit rates within the periphery group as a whole. It is hypothesized that while such new entry does provide some upper limit on the profit rates earned by periphery firms, such entry is not adequate to reduce the dispersion of periphery firm profit rates to a level comparable to that of core firm profit rates.[46]

One additional barrier to interindustry mobility which applies to all new entrants into the periphery sector of an industry is that the existence of intraindustry mobility barriers means that entry into the periphery sector of an industry is relatively risky. Entry by itself does not provide any assurance of earning the average prevailing rate of return. There is a wide range of possible performance results, and poor results are not easily remedied by a shift to a more profitable segment within the industry. Unlike core firms, periphery firms or newly formed firms do not in general have the resources to remedy mistakes or the ability to transform a low-profit position into a high-profit position.

Potential and actual competition from core firms both within and outside the industry provide some upper limit on periphery firm profitability, in addition to maintaining the spread between mean profit rates of core and periphery groups. In order for core firms to be interested on a simple profitability basis, the profit rate of a target periphery firm must be quite high relative to the mean profit rate among all periphery firms, plus offer the potential for profitable growth. Thus potential core firm takeovers do not provide systematic pressure which would tend to force periphery firm profit rates toward their mean.

Finally, the core–periphery hypothesis suggests that periphery entry into core-dominated industries has little significance

[46] Aggregate levels of new venture capital were approximately $100M per year during the years analyzed in the present study (1969-1974). Data from Venture Economics, Inc.

for core firm competitive conditions because, like the investment of periphery firms already in the industry, such entry
does not directly challenge core firms. The level of output provided by periphery firms is too small, their product line too
narrow, and the resources available for competition too limited. Barriers to entry which protect core firms' profitability
generally operate to limit intraindustry periphery firm expansion rather than to prevent all new periphery entry. Even substantial amounts of such entry are more likely to affect the
profit rate of established periphery firms than of core firms.
The argument is that competition in core-dominated industries is segmented; as a result, periphery firm entry does not
have the potential to affect core firm profitability on a systematic basis, although periphery firms may infrequently expand
to significant market share and core status.[47]

The core–periphery view is that because there is no systematic interaction, either actual or potential, between periphery
firms across the entire universe of periphery firms there is only
a weak tendency toward an equal rate of profit within the periphery. Further, there is no systematic interaction, either actual or potential, between core and periphery firms that would
create a strong tendency toward an equal profit rate across all
periphery firms. The centripetal forces on periphery firm profit
rates, while they exist, are significantly weaker than those operating on core firm profit rates. Thus, the hypothesis is that
periphery firms will have lower profits on average than core
firms and periphery firm profit rates will be significantly more
dispersed than core firm profit rates.

Summary

It is generally argued that the process of profit rate formation
in a competitive system also establishes a relation between risk
and rate of return across firms. Above-average risk associated

---

[47] Again Caves and Porter 1977 introduced the notion of such segmented
competition. Berry 1975, p. 144, provides some support for this hypothesis.

with a stream of profits represents a real cost to firms. In an industrial structure with generalized competition it is compensated at a rate that is more or less uniform across all firms, depending on the ease of capital flows.[48] Firms attempt to maximize risk-adjusted rates of return; they are indifferent between expected rates of return only when the associated risks are equal. According to this argument, in such an industrial structure competition tends to equalize risk-adjusted rates of return rather than simple rates of return across industries, and the result is a positive relation between the rate of return earned by firms and risk.

Just as profit rate formation in a competitive system involves more than the mean profit rate, it is proposed here that the process of profit rate formation in the core–periphery structure produces two rates of profit and two distinct relations between profit rate and risk. If risk is a function of both industry conditions and market power, then core firms' market power can offset some industry-specific risks and can help core firms to withstand the effects of such risks more successfully than periphery firms. Core firms' dominant position in an industry and their structural relation to the rest of the industry may force periphery firms to absorb a disproportionate share of any cyclical fluctuations. Core firm competitive tactics that may affect risk include selective vertical integration, establishment of a broader product line than that of periphery firms, better distribution systems, more intense advertising and marketing efforts, and cross-industry diversification.

However, the argument is that these tactics are not for the most part explicitly designed to reduce risk. Each of the tactics listed here is designed to achieve long-run profit maximization in competition with other core firms and periphery firms. These forms of competition, in the general context of corespective behavior, create the relatively stable environment for core firms that is required for long-run profit maximization. They also serve to assure high rates of profit and thus ample

[48] See, for example, Fisher and Hall 1969.

internal resources as well as access to external resources when needed.

Thus it is posited that the market power of core firms allows them to improve the terms of the expected tradeoff between risk and rate of return and to earn both higher and less risky profits than other firms. The simple relation between profit rates and risk is shaped by underlying structural forces, primarily the interacting effects of absolute firm size and dominance of particular markets. The successful pursuit of long-run profit maximization by core firms primarily via strategies defined by corespective behavior, allows them to outperform periphery firms on these two key dimensions of profitability, mean profit rate and risk. The proposed result is that there is no single underlying tradeoff with a single functional form between risk and rate of return; there are two.

The implications of this analysis differ from the implications of the usual industrial organization/neoclassical analysis of competition in two respects. The core–periphery analysis points to the formation of two distinct rates of profit as a result of two distinct but interrelated competitive processes. The usual analysis refers to a generalized process of competition which results in a single normal or average rate of return. Further, the core–periphery analysis suggests that it is large dominant firms, oligopolists, which engage in the most active interindustry competition, resulting in the formation of a rate of return which is relatively homogeneous and distinct from that formed by competition among smaller firms without significant market power. This, again, is in marked contrast to the usual analysis which suggests that the normal rate of return is determined by a competitive process among firms without significant market power. Firms with significant market power represent, in that view, isolated and atypical cases noteworthy precisely for that reason but with no relevance to formation of the average rate of return. Thus the usual analysis points to a homogeneous normal rate of return formed by a competitive process among firms without significant market power and a highly heterogeneous set of oligopoly profit rates which are determined by conditions in particular industries rather than any generalized competitive forces. This is precisely opposite the conclusion reached by core–periphery analysis.

EMPIRICAL HYPOTHESES

The preceding sections of this chapter provided a set of hypotheses about interfirm competition across core and periphery boundaries as well as industry boundaries, and a hypothesis about the relative positions of core and periphery firms in the economy. The basic hypothesis of this study can be summarized in empirical terms as: Core firms earn higher and less risky profit rates with lower intragroup variation than do periphery firms.

This broad empirical hypothesis can be subdivided into several testable hypotheses. The first such hypothesis is that core firms, defined as large firms in concentrated industries, earn higher profits than do all other firms. The argument is that core firms, because of their combined attributes of size and market power, have access to a range of profitable investments not available to other firms and compete in ways which do not in general lead to periphery-level profit rates. The forms of competition simultaneously result in entry barriers which further insulate core firms from intra- and interindustry competition. The concentration ratio is a proxy for the degree to which a small group of firms dominates an industry, or the joint market share of the dominant firms. Implicit in the hypothesis is that there is a critical level of the four-firm concentration ratio which, if exceeded, implies that the leading firms in the industry have sufficient market power to dominate the industry. If the level is lower the leading firms are not likely to be in such a position.

The second hypothesis is that there is significantly less variation in the profit rates earned by core firms as a group than exists in the group of periphery firms. The argument here is that core firms, because of their dominance of their home industries and their control over large quantities of capital, engage in an active process of interindustry competition that, together with potential competition, tends to equalize the rate of return earned across all core firms. Periphery firms by this argument tend to be isolated in market niches of various types and because of intraindustry constraints on their profitability, tend not to have the resources to engage in interindustry competition. In addition, even within an industry, because of their relatively small size and resultant specialization, periphery firms may face wide variation in business conditions and thus profitability. As a result of limited inter- as well as intraindustry competition between periphery firms there is less tendency toward the formation of a single periphery rate of profit.

The third hypothesis is that core firms earn profit rates which are significantly less risky than the profit rates earned by periphery firms; the simple relation between profit rates and the risk associated with them is shaped by structural forces underlying it, primarily the interacting effects of absolute size and market dominance.[49] This hypothesis has two subparts defined by two definitions of risk: temporal variation in profitability and the degree of financial leverage (the ratio of equity to assets). The first subhypothesis is that core firms earn both higher and less risky rates of return where risk is measured as temporal variability.

The argument is thus that the market power of core firms allows them to gain a more advantageous tradeoff between risk and rate of return in the following ways. Core firms may use selective integration within industries to reduce their own temporal sales and earnings fluctuations. Core firms may dominate the more stable segments of their industries and they may relegate more cyclically sensitive production to periphery firms. In addition, their distribution, marketing, and advertising expenditures tend to give core firms a demand stability advantage over small firms. The barriers to core entry created by core firm investment may also serve to isolate core firms from

---

[49] For further elaboration of the risk–return hypotheses typically found in the industrial organization literature see chapter five.

the intensified competition associated with cyclical downturns and thus may contribute to relative profit stability over time. Core firm advantages may also be reflected in a more favorable risk–return tradeoff than that faced by periphery firms.

The second subhypothesis is that core firms earn both higher and less risky rates of return where risk is measured as the ratio of equity to assets or leverage. The argument is that the degree of leverage chosen by a firm is a function of business risk mediated by market power. If firms choose their level of financial risk, measured by leverage, to partially offset their business risk then a firm with substantial business risk will choose a lower level of financial risk and thus a higher leverage ratio than a firm with less business risk. Core firms, because of their greater market power and thus reduced business risk, are expected to maintain capital structures with a lower ratio of equity to assets. Market power may also allow a more advantageous tradeoff between rate of return and leverage for core firms than for periphery firms.

CHAPTER THREE

The Development of Core and Periphery

THIS chapter outlines some key elements in the development of the core and periphery based on a set of details about the evolution of the industrial structure in the United States on which there is general agreement in the literature of economic history and industrial organization. The development analyzed is in two parts: the merger movement and subsequent consolidation of core firms, which extended from the late nineteenth century to the early 1920s; and the period beginning in the late 1920s and extending through the present, characterized by increasing core firm diversification.

THE FORMATION OF CORE AND PERIPHERY

The rationalization of the transportation system in the 1870s, signaled by real and steady declines in railroad freight rates, opened up the economy to a process of integration. Firms no longer isolated in local markets could now compete.[1] Competition between railroads, and between railroads and other forms of transport such as canal and ocean shipping contributed to the decline in transport costs.[2] Manufacturing firms began to compete in the greatly enlarged national market. Technical innovations allowed them to cut costs, expand production, and cut prices.[3] Some of the industries affected by real technical breakthroughs included sugar, oil, brewing, cig-

---

[1] Chandler 1977, pp. 207–239; V. Clark 1929, pp. 529–33; Cochran and Miller 1961, pp. 129–34; Kırkland 1961, pp. 75–76; Vatter 1975, pp. 193–94.

[2] Chandler 1977, pp. 188–89; Vatter 1975, p. 195.

[3] V. Clark 1929, pp. 168–69, 286–303; Kirkland 1961, pp. 163–80; Cochran and Miller 1961, pp. 135–40.

arettes, matches, flour, canned goods, iron and steel, sewing machines, and agricultural implements.[4]

These innovations were associated with an increase in the capital-intensity of production and an increase in the size of plants measured in both capitalization and in output. The average capital invested per manufacturing establishment almost doubled between 1879 and 1899.[5] Average value added per firm in manufacturing, mining, and construction rose substantially (51.3 percent) for the same period.[6] A variety of specific examples makes the point more vividly. The average annual production of blast furnaces in steel production rose from 5,000 tons in 1860 to 65,000 tons in 1899.[7] The annual output of a flour mill in the geographical center of flour production increased from 274 barrels in 1874 to 1,837 by the late 1880s. Normal output for an oil refinery rose from 700 barrels per week in the early 1860s to 500 barrels per day by 1870. The largest breweries' production jumped from 5,000 to 8,000 barrels per year in 1860 to over 100,000 by 1877 and 500,000 to 800,000 by 1895.[8]

Competition via innovations and cost-cutting led to larger plants and firms but it also led to fewer firms. Aggressive competition by innovating firms drove many other producers who did not or could not innovate into bankruptcy. In each of the industries mentioned above, the same pressures that led to larger output per plant and firm also led to a sharp decrease in the number of firms producing and to the establishment of a relatively small group of leading firms.[9] For the economy as a whole these forces produced a steady decline in the rate of increase of the total number of firms in business.[10]

[4] Chandler 1977, pp. 240–83.
[5] U.S. Bureau of the Census 1965, ser. P107–122, p. 683; ser. V20–30, pp. 912–13.
[6] Ibid., ser. F238–49, p. 239; ser. V20–30, pp. 912–13.
[7] Temin 1964, pp. 166–67.
[8] Chandler 1977, pp. 253, 256.
[9] Ibid., pp. 240–83.
[10] U.S. Bureau of the Census 1965, ser. V20–30, pp. 912–13.

Even the reduction in the number of firms in these industries did not mean that competition automatically slowed. In many cases competition continued undiminished. In the iron and steel industry, competition by cost-cutting technology forced, smaller producers out, increased industry production, and led to downward pressure on prices and profits. A handful of dominant producers, including Jones and Laughlin, Carnegie, The Colorado Fuel and Iron Company, and The Illinois Steel Company, continued to compete by expanding their production capacities, taking over smaller firms and cutting prices. The result was not the anticipated high rate of profit but instead a squeeze on profits and the prospect of continued destabilizing competition among the few dominant firms.[11]

The competitive pressures made expanded production and price-cutting general phenomena in much of manufacturing, resulting in a secular price decline across four severe business cycles (1873–1879, 1882–1885, 1893–1894, 1895–1897).[12] The consumer price index declined 34.4 percent between 1870 and 1900 while the wholesale price index showed a slightly larger decline of 39.3 percent. Price declines were largest for manufactured goods and particularly for producer goods.[13] In general, prices in 1869 were higher than in any following year up to World War I. This steady decline in prices was accompanied by a steady growth of production: GNP almost doubled between the decades of 1869–1879 and 1890–1900.[14] Value added in manufacturing more than doubled between 1869 and 1899; the annual increase was 7 percent. Value added in mining rose by about 260 percent for the same period or about 8.7 percent per year.[15]

As a result of these competitive pressures producers turned to collective action in an attempt to control production and

[11] Temin 1964; V. Clark 1929, pp. 286–303.

[12] Vatter 1975, p. 189.

[13] U.S. Bureau of the Census 1965, ser. E135–66, p. 211; ser. E52–63, p. 201.

[14] Ibid., Table F1–5, p. 224.

[15] Ibid., Table F238–49, p. 239.

prices. National "associations" and trade groups were an early response to declining prices, and by the 1880s they were widespread.[16] Their practices included price fixing, establishment of production quotas, and the allocation of markets to particular producers. Such loose consolidations predominated through the late 1890s but most of them failed to achieve any lasting solution to the problems of competition and instability. This structure of control had no means of enforcing the agreements, which therefore tended to be highly unstable, especially in cyclical downturns when pressure to maintain market share intensified. In addition, successful control over output and subsequent increases in profit rates created incentives for firms to break the agreement and increase production, for firms outside the group to increase production, and for new firms to enter the industry.[17] Although the trust form pioneered by Standard Oil Company provided the legal basis for real consolidation of production capacity and centralized control over operating and investment decisions, it did not become the dominant organizational response to the competitive pressures of the period.[18] There were only six successful trusts and two failures, and all eight were in the refining and distilling industries.[19]

A combination of political and economic changes allowed a permanent solution to the problem of "ruinous competition" not provided by such consolidations. The New Jersey general incorporation law passed in 1888-89 provided the legal structure necessary to carry out true consolidations rather than ad hoc agreements involving independent firms that had begun to face increased legal pressure under the Sherman Antitrust Act of 1890. A series of Supreme Court rulings between 1890 and 1899 made any combination of firms to influence prices or to

[16] Chandler 1977, p. 317.

[17] Ibid., pp. 317–18; V. Clark 1929, pp. 171–76, 277–86, 377–84; Cochran and Miller 1961, pp. 142–46; Kirkland 1961, pp. 199–203.

[18] Chandler 1977, p. 319; Cochran and Miller 1961, pp. 140–46; Kirkland 1961, pp. 203–206.

[19] Chandler 1977, pp. 320–21.

regulate production a clear violation of the Sherman Act. Thus pools, associations, trade groups, and cartels were all subject to prosecution, but the single corporation formed through merger was not. As a result the corporate form became the preferred and clearly legal form of consolidation.[20]

The formation of a market in industrial securities provided a source of funds not available from the low and fluctuating profits that characterized competing firms, which could be used to finance consolidation and expansion. This market had begun with limited public trading of trust "certificates" and matured during the 1893 to 1897 depression when the limited number of industrial preferred stocks outperformed most of the more accepted railroad stocks.[21] The introduction of combined preferred common stock offerings by industrial companies reduced the risk of holding industrials and was critical to the widespread acceptance by bankers and investors that followed. The funds supplied through stock sales were essential to carrying out the merger strategy for even the largest firms, which had most of their assets tied up in fixed capital.[22]

The 1898 to 1902 merger wave permitted by the removal of such institutional barriers was enormous. Between 25 and 30 percent of total manufacturing assets were involved over the five-year period.[23] Mergers involved 50 percent or more of total industry capital in five key industries: primary metals, transportation equipment, machinery, paper and allied products, and chemicals; and more than 40 percent in three additional industries: tobacco products, electrical machinery, and stone, clay, and glass products.[24] The preponderance of these mergers were horizontal and established small groups of large firms within most manufacturing industries.[25] This type of

---

[20] Bain 1951, pp. 625–27; Chandler 1959; Chandler 1977, pp. 331–33; Kirkland 1961, pp. 316–24; Letwin 1965, pp. 150–230; Thorelli 1954, pp. 440–500.

[21] Navin and Sears 1955, pp. 106, 126.

[22] Ibid., pp. 134–38; Nelson 1959, pp. 89–100.

[23] Nelson 1959, p. 37.

[24] Ibid., p. 171.

[25] Moody 1904, pp. 485–87.

consolidation was quantitatively more important in this initial merger wave than in any subsequent one. The mean number of firms per merger was nine, while 26.3 percent of all mergers involved ten or more firms.[26] The immediate effect of all this activity was a radical transformation of the industrial structure in manufacturing.[27]

Not all the newly merged firms survived. The pattern of successes and failures provides some clues to the real bases of the merger movement and of the emergent dominance of core firms. The traditional view is that successful mergers and huge firms were the result of an interaction between technology and market size. Real economies of scale could only be realized by firms that were so large relative to the market that technical efficiency implied an oligopolistic market structure. According to this view, mergers succeeded where there were real economies of scale and they failed where these were not present. The net result was interpreted as an overall increase in economic efficiency as well as an increase in the concentration of economic power.[28]

Yet, there is no clear evidence that mergers had anything to do with economies of scale in production. The firms which competed in the 1890s were themselves the result of a competitive process which had winnowed out many of the inefficient producers; a large number of these firms had already realized production economies. There is no reason to think that the size of the newly merged firms was required to realize these economies and there is some positive evidence that mergers did not result in production economies at all.

A careful review of the scanty evidence on the question by Richard Edwards indicates that "generally plant size had increased sufficiently before the turn-of-the-century mergers to realize all technological economies of scale." Many if not all of the large consolidated firms in industries including steel, electrical manufacturing, and agricultural implements continued

[26] Nelson 1959, p. 54.
[27] Bain 1951, pp. 616–19.
[28] Ibid., pp. 617–20; Kolko 1963, pp. 12–17.

after consolidation to operate most of the plants used by individual firms prior to the mergers. Limited statistical evidence on plant size and concentration "indicates that in ten of the eleven industries the turn-of-the-century consolidation extended far beyond what was required to achieve technical efficiency."[29] Finally, analysis of the postmerger performance of consolidated firms shows that firms classified in 1904 as having monopoly control in their markets were significantly more successful than those that did not have such control, that is, market control was significantly related to success.[30]

Alfred Chandler also argues that horizontal combinations in pursuit of market power were not adequate to ensure success and that economies in production did not exist at such a scale either to justify the existence of the huge corporations or to protect them from a new wave of competition.[31] Many of the merged companies did not succeed. Those that did moved beyond the merger strategy to consolidate and protect their new market positions.[32] The success of such companies, which is attributed to efficiency, is more plausibly attributed to the successful control of prices and production. A large number of mergers failed precisely because they did not successfully develop real market power.

Although some failed, many newly merged firms successfully consolidated their positions. A transformed industrial structure dominated by core firms ensconced in most manufacturing industries emerged by the latter half of the 1910s.

EXTENSION OF CORE DOMINANCE

Diversification

The limited available evidence on historical patterns of diversification is consistent with the theory of core and periphery.

[29] R. Edwards 1979, p. 218.
[30] Ibid., p. 219.
[31] Chandler 1977.
[32] Ibid., R. Edwards 1979; Kolko 1963; Livermore 1935.

In particular the evidence is consistent with the argument that core firms diversified after outgrowing their home industries. Such diversification resulted in intracore competition and in the establishment of new bastions of market power with associated high rates of return.

The late 1920s marked a decisive switch in the basic competitive strategy of core firms, from vertical integration and consolidation of market power, to diversification in search of profitable new markets.[33] Although a majority of core firms in 1919 were vertically integrated, especially those in concentrated industries, virtually none was diversified. By 1929 a significant proportion of the largest firms were diversified and this trend has continued and accelerated. Further, very few core firms pursued a strategy of vertical integration after 1929. In fact, the proportion of vertically integrated core firms may have declined between 1929 and 1959.[34] Apart from a small group of firms identified by Richard Rumelt which joined the core early, pursued vertical integration, and failed to diversify extensively, core firms all began to diversify.[35]

Richard Rumelt's analysis of diversification by the top 500 manufacturing firms (based on detailed product line information over a twenty-year period, 1949 to 1969) provides substantial evidence of the increase in dominant firm diversification. The proportion of large firms that relied principally on a single industry dropped precipitously over this period. Almost exclusively, it has been core firms which have diversified. In 1954 less than 1 percent of all firms were diversified, yet they provided about 40 percent of the jobs in manufacturing and mining.[36]

[33] Chandler 1969, pp. 255–98.

[34] Gort 1962, p. 27.

[35] Rumelt 1974. Rumelt's argument that these firms have performed significantly less well suffers from a poorly chosen sample. For example, his sample of petroleum companies excludes three of the top eight domestic companies and includes several that are not in the top fifteen. Thus he mixes the poor performance of periphery firms in these industries with the continued good performance of core firms.

[36] Gort 1962, p. 27.

The core–periphery theory suggests that core firms diversified in order to escape pressures which were a direct result of
their earlier successes; once such firms succeeded in establishing integrated market power they began to face a shortage of
investment outlets. When desired firm growth rates exceeded
the growth rate of industry demand, it is hypothesized that
core firms in concentrated industries did not have the option of
increasing their market share by growing faster than the industry. To do so would have jeopardized industry stability, only
recently established, and thus the basis of core firms' profitability.

Evidence from two large-scale historical statistical investi-
gations supports a characterization of diversifying firms' home
industries which is consistent with the core–periphery view.
Alfred Chandler shows that the large integrated firms of the
early 1920s were overwhelmingly in highly concentrated industries.[37] Michael Gort demonstrates, in addition, that large
firms in concentrated industries were significantly more likely
to diversify than those in less-concentrated industries. Gort
also finds a significant positive relationship between average
firm size in an industry and the degree to which firms in the industry diversified; and a significant negative relationship between industry growth and the extent to which firms in the industry diversified.[38] Thus diversification was generally by large
firms located in concentrated industries, that is, core firms,
where firm growth probably exceeded industry growth.

Available evidence also suggests a picture of entered industries which is consistent with the goals of profit-maximizing
core firms attempting to escape the confines of limited investment potential in their home industries. Core firms have diversified into industries with characteristics which allowed them,
at least temporarily, to circumvent the structural problems in
their home industry. The new industries tended to have high
growth, advanced technology, and high rates of growth in la-

[37] Chandler 1969, p. 262.
[38] Gort 1962, pp. 135–41.

bor productivity.[39] Core firms, based in industries which were similarly technologically advanced and which had required investment in technical expertise, made the transition to the new industries more easily.

The historical pattern of diversification has, however, underscored the significance of core firms' bases in particular oligopolistic industries with high barriers to entry. While diversification represents a form of core firm competition, it is competition based in a secure market position in a particular industry or industries and it depends on an identifiable set of skills and expertise not easily generalizable to any industry. This provides a limit to intracore competition, and the historically conservative pattern of diversification stands in contrast to the theories of large firm competition proffered by some authors.[40]

Diversifying firms have tended to move into industries closely related in a technical sense to their home industry or into industries which required similar resources and expertise.[41] Studies of diversification that have relied on product counts have tended to overstate the amount and the extent of diversification. In Gort's study, for example, nearly half of the total "product additions" by the top 111 firms represented, in each case, less than 2 percent of the firm's output.[42] This does not mean that such new production is not potentially significant for the firm, but it does overstate the degree to which core firms have moved into new industries.

Although Rumelt's analysis shows increased diversification by the largest firms the trend was toward only a moderately diversified posture. In Rumelt's diversification categories (which are based on the proportion of sales from an industry or group of related industries) the proportion of firms that diversified by relating new businesses to existing skills and resources showed the largest increase while firms that diversified into unrelated

[39] Ibid., pp. 103–130.
[40] Clifton 1975; Semmler 1984.
[41] Gort 1962; Rumelt 1974, pp. 47–78.
[42] Gort 1962, p. 35.

industries showed the smallest increase and was the smallest category in absolute size, after single industry firms, in 1969. Only about 2 percent of these firms had entered the category of "acquisitive conglomerate" by 1969.[43]

A moderate diversification strategy appears to have successfully resolved the reinvestment problems of core firms. Core firms that pursued the more conservative strategies earned the highest rates of return of all the subgroups of the top 500 firms. These firms also had the highest growth rates and were superior in all other performance measures.[44] The moderate diversification strategy was superior both to more extreme diversification strategies and to the no diversification strategy.

The hypothesis that cyclical risk-spreading is a primary diversification goal is contradicted by the limited evidence. Firms seem to diversify into industries more cyclically sensitive than their home industries.[45] In addition, firms that pursue a moderate diversification strategy show less temporal variability in earnings than firms pursuing any other strategy.[46]

Core firms have entered new industries in pursuit of profits and growth that were no longer available in their home industries. The limited evidence is consistent with the core–periphery analysis of competition, that core firms' expansion led to competition both with other diversifying core firms and with periphery firms. Gort's data suggest that core firms diversified into industries with other core firms among the leading producers, as well as into "periphery industries" populated primarily by small firms. Large firms frequently diversified into

[43] Rumelt 1974, pp. 47–78.
[44] Ibid., p. 94.
[45] Gort 1962, pp. 114–17.
[46] Rumelt 1974, pp. 102–103; Berry 1975, and others have shown that there is not a strong ex post relationship between profitability and diversification. This is consistent with the core–periphery explanation for diversification as an investment outlet from pressures within home industries. The marginal (especially short-run) profit rate might well be lower than the average firm profit rate in new diversification efforts but from the core–periphery perspective this profit rate is not a meaningful measure of the success of a diversification strategy.

industries characterized by high levels of concentration, by high capital requirement barriers to entry and by large average plant size.[47] William Shepherd's evidence suggests that large firm diversification has occurred primarily in the moderate to low range of concentration and only infrequently in "highly concentrated" (concentration greater than 70 percent) industries, and that this diversification was inversely related to the concentration level in entered industries.[48] These apparently divergent bits of evidence are consistent with the hypothesis that while there is significant interindustry intracore competition, this competition is less common in the basic home industries of core firms when they exhibit very high levels of concentration. Gort's industry data are at the four-digit level while Shepherd's data are at the two-digit level. Large firms frequently have a leading role in narrowly defined four-digit industries with relatively high levels of concentration, but these industries often do not represent the basic home industry of the firm.[49] The broader two-digit industry classification probably captures large firm dominance, which may include substantial market share in several four-digit industries, more consistently and thus two-digit industries with high levels of concentration are more likely to represent the home industry of large firms than four-digit industries with similar levels of concentration.

Shepherd's analysis of the performance of thirty-five "consensus oligopolies," or industries generally agreed to be oligopolies, over the postwar period provides further relevant evidence. Between 1947 and 1966 there was no significant change in concentration (greater than 10 percentage points overall) in twenty-nine of the thirty-five industries. There were four significant increases versus two declines, neither of which indicated a real decline in concentration. Shepherd's conclusion is that oligopoly power, once established, does not dissi-

[47] Gort 1962, pp. 103–130.
[48] Shepherd 1970, pp. 140–44.
[49] Ibid., p. 142.

pate.[50] Although intracore competition does take place, when outside core firms invade the bastions of other core firms' power that market power is not substantially affected.

Core firms have tended not to confront other core firms where concentration is very high but some evidence suggests that intracore competition has nonetheless been widespread. In 1963 about one-quarter of the employees of the top 200 firms were in industries outside the firms' major (two-digit) industry. In each of the two-digit industry groups the number of companies from the top 200 based primarily in another industry greatly outnumbered the number of top 200 companies based primarily in that industry. On average, there were six times as many of the top 200 companies based outside the industry as those based in the industry.[51] Although the two-digit or major industry group is a broad unit of analysis, the diversification suggested by these data is consistent with interaction between core firms based in different industries. While it is possible that firms within a two-digit industry do not have significant interactions, interaction by core firms based within a two-digit industry is also possible.

Finally, core firm diversification led to the extension of market power by large firms from their home industries into new industries. A large proportion of such efforts were successful. Core firms diversified into many industries in a fairly substantial way, that is, where production of the new product is primary to at least one plant. In about a third of such cases core firms assumed a leading position (top eight) within a relatively short time (twelve years on average). The proportion of leading positions gained rose with time. Of the leading positions taken, more than half were positions in the top four.[52] There is no direct evidence on the characteristics of the firms which were displaced by such entry. However, all of the entry into leading positions in Gort's sample could easily have taken

[50] Ibid., p. 118.

[51] Ibid., pp. 80–83; U.S. Congress, Senate, Subcommittee on Antitrust and Monopoly 1964.

[52] Gort 1962, pp. 128–30.

place without displacing a single core firm. Since there were approximately 200 industry groups, there were 1,600 leading positions, while only 376 product additions primary to at least one plant were made by the top 111 firms.[53]

The aggregate result of core firm diversification has been a significant expansion of market power by core firms. In 1950, early in the postwar push to diversify, divisions of at least one of the top 1,000 firms were among the four largest producers in more than a quarter of the 1,014 four-digit industries, despite the fact that the product was not the firm's primary product and that the division's output constituted less than 10 percent of the firm's total output. In 1958 such divisions of the top 100 firms were among the top four in more than half of all four-digit industries. At the same time, divisions of the top 100 firms were ranked between fifth and eighth largest producers, while not represented among the top four, in less than 10 percent of these industries. Similar results held in 1963.[54] Finally, in 1963 firms classified elsewhere but ranked in the industry's top eight firms produced one-third or more of total output in 44 percent of all four-digit industries. In 17 percent of these industries such firms produced two-thirds or more of industry output.[55] In a quarter of concentrated four-digit industries (four-firm concentration ratio greater than 50 percent) 50 percent or more of the top eight firms' output was produced by firms classified elsewhere.[56]

Trends in Concentration

The limited evidence on long-term trends in both aggregate and industry concentration is consistent with the core–periphery view of the gradual expansion of core firm dominance.

The first study to estimate aggregate concentration trends was that of Gardiner Means, who found that the growth rate

[53] Ibid.
[54] Shepherd 1970, p. 141.
[55] Blair 1972, p. 57.
[56] Shepherd 1970, pp. 141–42.

of assets of the 200 largest nonfinancial corporations exceeded that of all nonfinancial corporations and that this difference increased significantly between 1924 and 1929.[57] In a later study of the period 1929 to 1933, Means's calculations showed that the share of total assets of all nonfinancial corporations held by the top 200 such corporations grew significantly, and that the increase occurred between 1929 and 1931 though there was a slight decline between 1931 and 1933.[58]

An article by Morris Adelman was the next significant attempt to address the question. Adelman concurred that aggregate concentration as measured by Means clearly rose between 1909 and 1933. He also noted that the increases between 1929 and 1933 and between 1924 and 1929 were especially clear.[59] Norman Collins and Lee Preston calculated the aggregate concentration trend for the 1909 to 1958 period using the assets of the largest 100 firms in manufacturing, mining, and distribution as a proportion of all such firms. Their figures for 1909 to 1929 also support the thesis that aggregate concentration grew substantially during the period.[60]

The only study, in fact, that does not show this increase is that of A.D.H. Kaplan. His estimates are for approximately the same universe as that treated by Collins and Preston, yet his estimate for the share of the top 100 industrial corporations in 1909 is 26.0 percent as compared to the 17.7 percent estimate of Collins and Preston.[61] It is this difference in base-year concentration that is the source of Kaplan's finding of no significant upward trend. The 1909 base period is a misleading one from which to begin an analysis of the long-term trend in aggregate concentration, because it follows the merger wave so closely and reflects the "effronteries of promoters" as much as any real market power.[62] Kaplan does not calculate an aggregate concentration figure between 1909 and 1929 but if a

[57] Berle and Means 1932.
[58] Means 1965.
[59] Adelman 1951, pp. 269–96.
[60] Collins and Preston 1961, pp. 986–1003.
[61] Kaplan 1954.
[62] This point is made by R. Edwards 1975.

postconsolidation date is chosen, the first is 1929, then his data also show a steady upward trend through 1960.[63]

The movement of the trend in the period between 1931 and 1947 to 1950 is subject to slightly more contention. Adelman's estimates of the trend between 1931 and 1947 showed a clear divergence from the trend since 1909 and from that which had been extrapolated forward by Berle and Means. His adjusted figures actually showed a decline in aggregate concentration but his conclusion was only that the tendency to increasing concentration in manufacturing probably did not exist for this period.[64]

Edward Mason noted certain problems with Adelman's estimates, for example, that the prolonged upswing after the depression favored the growth of small firms and that large firms "wrote down" the value of their assets more actively than small firms during the depression. However, Mason concluded that forces tending to disperse asset concentration in manufacturing reasserted themselves in this period and that the earlier trend toward increasing concentration did not represent the operation of natural law.[65]

Means's review reached basically the same conclusion. While he rejects, with Mason, Adelman's estimate of a decline over the period, he argued that there is no basis for arguing that aggregate concentration increased for nonfinancial corporations.[66] The clear increase from 1929 to 1933 was a result of the depression and did not continue through the recovery and World War II.

The general trend of aggregate concentration for manufacturing since 1947 is not disputed. The specification of the trend relies on data generated by the Census Bureau which is substantially superior to that on which earlier estimates were based. The exact level and the precise percentage changes in aggregate concentration vary with definitions of size and the relevant group of top corporations, but it is agreed by most an-

[63] Kaplan 1954.
[64] Adelman 1951.
[65] Mason 1957.
[66] Means 1965.

alysts that aggregate concentration in the manufacturing sector has increased substantially since 1947 and that several subtrends are discernible within the general increase. A sharp increase occurred between 1947 and 1954 and a more gradual increase has followed since that time. Aggregate concentration increased during the 1960s but the trend appears to have flattened during the 1970s. Exact comparison of post-1972 data with pre-1972 data is made more difficult by changes in the method the Federal Trade Commission uses to calculate the series.[67] Given the data difficulties and the relatively short period of the 1970s for which data is available, it is probably safe to say that the upward trend in aggregate concentration has flattened for the early 1970s.[68]

To summarize briefly, there is general agreement that aggregate concentration, or, the proportion of all nonfinancial assets owned by the top 100 or 200 nonfinancial corporations, grew substantially, about 40 percent, between 1909 and 1929; that the sharp increase between 1929 and 1931 was a short-run phenomenon; that aggregate concentration did not grow much if at all between 1929 and the late 1940s; and that the upward trend resumed after 1947 but flattened in the early 1970s. Overall there has been a clear upward trend in aggregate concentration over this century.

The trend in postwar levels of industry or "market" concentration can be evaluated in several ways. The first and most direct is the calculation of an average industry concentration ratio in each year for which data is available. A simple average can be calculated, or industry size can be taken into account through an average weighted by industry employment or value of shipments. Since the underlying data has been published by the Census Bureau at fairly regular intervals since 1947, estimates based on published industry concentration ratios have a degree of uniformity.[69] A major problem with industry ratios compared over a substantial time is that industry definitions

[67] Penn 1976.
[68] Scherer 1980, p. 48.
[69] Allen 1976; Bain 1968; Mueller and Hamm 1974; Scherer 1980; Shepherd 1964; U.S. Federal Trade Commission 1969.

change and as a result, only those industries with comparable definitions across the whole period can be used. It has been alleged that this introduces sample bias by removing the most dynamic industries, the ones most likely to show concentration decreases. Several attempts to test for the bias failed to show any.[70] Despite some cyclical movement, weighted average industrial concentration has shown a weak positive trend since 1947. Willard Mueller and Larry Hamm estimated that average concentration increased by 3.9 percentage points, or by about 10 percent, between 1947 and 1970.[71] The estimates of Bruce Allen are comparable.[72]

Another method used to evaluate average concentration analyzes the distribution of employment by industry concentration ratios. This measure shows fairly steady declines in the proportion of employment in industries with four-firm concentration ratios over 50 percent, although this is not the case for all industries with concentration at 40 percent or more.[73] The problem with the employment measure is that more concentrated industries tend to have more rapidly rising capital–labor ratios, resulting in a downward bias in measured concentration.

A third technique compares the number of industries registering concentration increases with those registering declines. For four-digit industries between 1947 and 1966 more industries registered increases in concentration than declines.[74]

In summary, the core group of firms emerged from a combination of forces in the last third of the nineteenth century and was consolidated by the early 1920s. If the core group was to maintain its position in a growing economy, core firms had to expand at least as fast as their home industries. Since these firms were very large compared to all firms and since the industries they dominated were large, capital-intensive industries central to the industrialization process, maintenance of

[70] U.S. Federal Trade Commission 1969; Weston and Ornstein 1973.
[71] Mueller and Hamm 1974.
[72] Allen 1976.
[73] Shepherd 1964; Weston and Ornstein 1973.
[74] Blair 1972.

position in their home industries seemed to imply at least a constant aggregate asset share. These characteristics, plus core firms' attempts to increase their market share, to integrate forward and backward, and to diversify, seemed to imply a rising aggregate share. The evidence, such as it is, on aggregate concentration trends between 1909 and 1929 is consistent with this hypothesis.

The sharp rise in aggregate concentration between 1929 and 1931 as the depression struck and the constancy or slow increase in aggregate share through World War II suggest that core firms managed to maintain their position in the economy during this fifteen-year period despite a series of economic upheavals.

The story since the war is based on somewhat better evidence. It suggests a continuation of core firm dominance and a further extension of that dominance. An important part of the story is the divergence between the steadily increasing aggregate asset share of the top 200 firms and the relative constancy of average industrial concentration. This divergence is consistent with the view of core and periphery development since the 1920s. Core firms continued to grow and expand but did so outside their home industries. Core firms also made investments outside the U.S. economy, in foreign markets. Thus, core firms continued to increase their aggregate share of assets in the economy while failing to increase market shares within their home industries. It is possible that high growth rates in concentrated, capital-intensive industries could have outweighed concentration stability and resulted in increased aggregate concentration, but the evidence does not support this interpretation.

Stability of Core Membership

Measures of aggregate concentration provide information on the asset share of the top firms but leave unexamined the identity of the firms and the distribution of assets among them. A series of studies on the turnover among the largest firms were designed to meet this failing. The studies construct lists of the top 100 or 500 firms at roughly ten-year intervals since the merger wave of 1902. Turnover occurs when the identities of the top firms change.

A.D.H. Kaplan's was the first postwar analysis of turnover and it provoked both methodological criticism and a new series of studies of turnover. Kaplan's figures showed that only 30 to 40 of the top 100 corporations in 1909 survived until 1960, and he concluded that turnover was high.[75]

Critics at the time and since have noted a range of serious problems with Kaplan's definition of a firm's disappearance.[76] He simply lumped together all firm disappearances and left unmentioned important distinctions between types of disappearances, including those that occurred through the merger of two firms on the list, as a result of judicial antitrust proceedings, through the decline of industries, and when firms dropped off the top 100 list but continued as large corporations. By the crude turnover measure, a merger between two firms in the top 100 increases turnover but this can hardly be taken as evidence that large firms' position is eroding or unstable. In the postconsolidation period data from all the major turnover studies show that from two-thirds to three-quarters of total exits were the result of merger. Further, a firm which leaves the top 100 list but continues as a large firm relative to all firms in the economy and as a dominant firm in its home industry cannot be considered the equivalent of a firm which is liquidated. The breakup of firms by antitrust actions is not indicative of underlying economic forces; such firms certainly should not be classed with actual failures.

Seymour Friedland studied the previous experience and subsequent fates of entrants to and exits from his list of the top 50 firms between 1906 and 1950. He reported that entrants to the top 50 had generally been large firms for a considerable time and that a large proportion of firms that left the top 100 con-

[75] Kaplan 1954.
[76] Collins and Preston 1961; R. Edwards 1975.

tinued as large firms through the end of the period analyzed.[77] M. A. Adelman points out that many of the entries and exits can be explained in terms of the rise and fall of industries or changes in the broad structure of industries, even while firms retain their intraindustry importance. He estimates that of a total of 69 disappearances from the top 100 between 1909 and 1948, 46 can be explained in this way, while only 16 were the result of actual company failure. [78] Edwards demonstrates that when turnover is broken down by cause only 10 of the top 100 firms exited between 1919 and 1969 because they failed to grow or were liquidated. This is the equivalent of 0.2 firms per year or one firm every five years. Even when exits by merger are included, the total exit rate is only 0.8 firms per year.[79] As George Stigler put it for his slightly higher calculated failure rate of 1.0 firms per year, "once on the list, a company will, on the average, stay there for a century."[80]

A separate and equally critical question, addressed explicitly only by Richard Edwards, is that of the appropriate base year for studies of turnover among the top firms. Edwards argues that the status of the large firms formed in the last part of the nineteenth century and particularly during the merger wave was not consolidated until around 1920. Thus, analyses that measure turnover from some year prior to 1920 (or 1917) include turnover during the unstable period before 1920, which is not relevant to the question of whether large corporations, once their position was consolidated, continued to hold a dominant position in the U.S. economy.[81]

The analyses of several other authors also show a trend toward greater stability among large firms. Even using Kaplan's methods for defining entry to and exit from the top 100, they show that turnover among the top firms is declining significantly over time and that turnover is concentrated among the bottom 20 percent of the list. Edwards calculates separate fail-

[77] Friedland 1957.
[78] Adelman 1951.
[79] R. Edwards 1975.
[80] Stigler 1956.
[81] R. Edwards 1975.

ure rates, using Kaplan's method for his own data as well as that from the other major turnover studies, for the 1909 to 1919 period and for the post-1917 period. Data from all his studies show a dramatic decline in turnover for the later period from approximately 3.8 firms per year to approximately 1.1 firms per year.[82]

Finally, there is some further evidence on the relationship of stability to size. Thomas Navin constructed a list of the top 500 firms in 1917. He noted that turnover between 1917 and 1967 was concentrated primarily among the bottom 460 firms.[83] Edwards, using Navin's data, shows that of the bottom 200 firms, 40 were liquidated during the period while only 5 of the top 100 firms suffered that fate.[84] (In 1919 the top 100 firms were probably core firms while the bottom 200 of the top 500 list were probably not.) Stanley Boyle and Joseph McKenna also show that the frequency of exit is negatively related to firm size.[85]

Additional evidence on the stability of core firms is provided by a series of studies on the size distribution and rank ordering of large firms. Changes in the size distribution of the top firms as measured by shifts in the Lorenz curve for this group indicate the relative equality in size of the top firms, changes in that equality over time, and provide some indication of whether a subgroup controls a disproportionate share of the assets of the top firms or whether there is a tendency toward or away from such control over time. Collins and Preston construct Lorenz curves for the top 100 industrial corporations for the period 1909 to 1958. The curves show inequality among the top firms (the top 25 firms control over 50 percent of the assets) and relative stability over the fifty-year span, with a slight trend toward increasing equality.[86]

Changes in rank and size order of the top firms have been

[82] Boyle and McKenna 1970; Collins and Preston 1961; Friedland 1957; Stigler 1956.

[83] Navin 1970.

[84] R. Edwards 1975.

[85] Boyle and McKenna 1970.

[86] Collins and Preston 1961.

measured in several ways. Collins and Preston calculate the correlation coefficients between firm rankings and between the logarithms of asset size. Both sets of coefficients show increases over the 1909 to 1958 period, indicating that surviving firms "show a greater stability of size position in the last two periods than in the first two."[87] Ronald Bond also calculated correlation coefficients between logarithms of asset size. For surviving firms alone he found that for the period 1948 to 1968 the correlation coefficients were extremely stable over the whole period and that the level of correlation was comparable to that of Collins and Preston.[88]

David Mermelstein regresses survivor asset shares on their base year shares for ten-year intervals between 1909 and 1964. (Asset share is defined to be the firm's share of total surviving firms' assets in each benchmark year.) The regression coefficients, which are used as the measure of the stability of shares over the intervals, show an upward trend over the whole time with a peak in the 1948 to 1958 period. Thus large firms in the later periods were more likely to hold onto their shares than large firms earlier in the century.[89]

Bond uses the correlation coefficient technique of Collins and Preston but he corrects for two drawbacks of earlier studies. He analyzes all 200 top firms in every year rather than just survivors in order to understand mobility patterns for all top firms. He also explicitly adjusts for the effects of mergers, both acquisitions and losses, in order to calculate the effect of mergers on observed mobility. He found that observed mobility rose sharply when all top 200 firms were included. But when he adjusted the figures to remove the effects of mergers, most of that increase in mobility disappeared. Measuring mobility by changes in asset rank for all 200 firms in each of four periods between 1948 and 1968, he shows that mobility is stable and that apparent increases in mobility were the result of

[87] Ibid.
[88] Bond 1975.
[89] Mermelstein 1969.

mergers, which had precisely the opposite effect. They increased the centralization of economic activity.[90]

Evidence on the stability of the largest firms in the economy, a group which is roughly synonymous with the core, is consistent with the view that once established, the probability of failure or even decline for a core firm is almost negligible. Core firms are almost, as Robert Averitt suggested, eternal.

COMPETITION AND MONOPOLY

Several studies have attempted to categorize all industries as either effectively competitive or broadly monopolistic.[91] The most recent study, by Shepherd, argues that the U.S. economy became significantly more competitive between 1958 and 1980. He reaches that conclusion on the basis of structural and performance indicators by four-digit industry that suggest, in Shepherd's view, that a substantial number of industries have moved into the "effectively competitive" category from the "monopoly" categories. This finding is supported for the manufacturing sector in particular which is the area of relevance to this study.[92]

Shepherd's analysis is within the industrial organization tradition, which differs in its analytical approach from the core–periphery theory.[93] Analyses that segment industries into competitive and monopoly groups are not directed to the same question addressed by the core–periphery analysis and reflect in part the single-industry focus of much work in the industrial organization area. In the core–periphery view, the firm is the unit of analysis rather than the industry. In addition it is the core–periphery hypothesis that core firms compete more actively than periphery firms, precisely opposite the view embod-

[90] Bond 1975.

[91] Kaysen and Turner 1959; Nutter and Einhorn 1969; Stigler 1950; Wilcox 1940.

[92] Shepherd 1982.

[93] See chapters two, four, and five for more analysis of the industrial organization tradition.

ied in the competition–monopoly studies that firms in industries with structural evidence of monopoly power compete significantly less actively than other firms. Further, core firms have from their beginning been aggressive competitors in international markets.

It appears that most of the increased competition in manufacturing found in Shepherd's study is the result of import-related structural change and deteriorating performance measures, and that the latter were critical in the recategorization. Whether this is an adequate basis for the study's strong conclusions is doubtful, at least with respect to manufacturing. It should be noted that the bulk of the changes recorded by Shepherd probably occurred between 1970 and 1980 and that some of the more significant in the manufacturing sector can probably be assigned even more narrowly to the latter half of the decade. While it has been generally observed that the U.S. economy is undergoing a period of structural change, which began some time in the early to middle 1970s, it may be misleading to focus on performance measures during a period of instability to establish the endpoint of an historical series extending back over thirty years, particularly when drawing broad conclusions about trends in the level of competition that prevail in the economy.

In the core–periphery hypothesis, core membership is defined by a combination of industry structural characteristics and the relative size of the firm in the universe of all firms. Performance is an implication of core membership, not a criterion for membership. Further, while most competition is held to be the result of core firm activities, this competition does not have the normative implications of competition in the usual sense of microeconomic theory. In order for there to be an economy-wide increase in competition in a normative sense from the core–periphery perspective there would have to be a crosscyclical decline in the profit rate and risk differential between core and periphery firms, both on an intra- and an interindustry basis. In structural terms, the size of the core group would have to shrink substantially.

The industry categorization approach assumes effectively that intraindustry dynamics are unimportant. From the core–periphery perspective intraindustry profit rate differentials are important; the intraindustry pattern of performance has implications for the effect of new external competition on the nature of intraindustry competition. It would be surprising if small firms were not hurt as badly or worse than large firms, thus leaving intraindustry performance differentials intact and blunting somewhat the claim of increased competition from a domestic firm perspective.

The difference in approach can be summarized using the automobile industry as an example. Shepherd indicates that the industry moved into the "competitive" group primarily as a result of performance measures; structural measures alone dictated that the industry remain in the "monopoly" group. From the core–periphery perspective, the dominant firms in the industry remain core firms. Though in the late 1970s and early 1980s each of those dominant firms has undergone varying degrees of deterioration in performance and undertaken different types of competitive response, each has, to date, successfully dealt with the crisis that faced them individually and the domestic industry as a whole.[94] While it is unusual for outside core firms to enter a core-dominated industry like the auto industry, it can happen if the profit opportunities exist. Foreign competitors in the domestic auto market can be usefully viewed as new core firm entrants, although these foreign firms are quite different in some respects than other potential core firm entrants in that they developed large-scale industry-specific expertise and market power in a somewhat protected setting before entering the U.S. auto market. It is also possible that core firms could fail in the face of such competition, but core firms are well suited to meet it successfully.

Shepherd suggests that import competition has caused a "shift toward cost-based pricing" and has therefore "intro-

[94] See, for example, *The Wall Street Journal*, 4 October 1984, p. 55; *Value Line*, 28 September 1984, pp. 100–125.

duced a marked change toward the competitive outcome."[95] In the core–periphery view even dramatic short-term declines in profitability during such a change in the structure of intra-industry competition have no necessary implications for the longer-term success of the affected firms or for the level of domination by core firms. Insofar as part of the success of the new competitive thrust is a result of technology-related cost advantages, then domestic core firms may be expected to adopt the new technology. Whether this will result in a long-term reduction in profit rates for domestic or foreign-based core firms is doubtful.

In the core–periphery view, while U.S.-based core firms have always competed actively, the period of the 1970s clearly marked a significant change in the nature of competition within many industries and in the nature of the required competitive response. If a global restructuring of the automobile industry is occurring, then core firms may be expected to and, in fact, are responding to the competitive pressures. Any analysis of intraindustry competition must now take account of the foreign entrants as industry members rather than focus solely on U.S.-based firms. As an extreme example, even if domestic firms were reduced to marginal status in the domestic market the result would not necessarily be described as more competitive. Core firm status could be assumed by foreign producers without any necessary net gains in competition. Despite the fact that U.S. firms have lost significant domestic market share there is no evidence that overall (including foreign firms) core firm profit rates in the industry have fallen on a long-term basis.[96]

In addition, top U.S. auto manufacturers are making significant headway in penetrating the European market and are entering into a variety of long-term production and marketing agreements with Japanese firms designed to forestall further erosion in domestic and world market share.[97] The ultimate

[95] Shepherd 1982, p. 622.

[96] *Value Line*, 28 September 1984.

[97] See, for example, *Barron's*, 1 October 1984, "The Colonies Strike Back."

outcome will be an industry defined on a worldwide basis and, in the core–periphery view, one dominated by core firms also defined on a worldwide basis. There will certainly be at least two U.S.-based firms among that group.

While the core–periphery hypothesis is oriented toward the domestic U.S. economy and patterns of competition within it, it is expected that the evolution of a more integrated world economy will produce a similar evolution at that level as occurred within the U.S. The ultimate role of U.S. core firms will be determined by their competitive response. Nonetheless such firms are in a significantly better position to meet that competition than are periphery firms.

In the competition-monopoly view, the new foreign competition is inconsistent with a "monopoly" position and is suggestive of a restructuring of the affected industries on a more competitive, in the normative sense, basis. The core–periphery view is that intracore competition is expected, represents the usual pattern of competition, and is consistent with ongoing core firm domination of particular industries, albeit with the possible addition of several new core members, and therefore superior profit performance. While recent incursions by foreign producers represent a significant change in the intensity of competition in some industries, such competition does not by itself suggest that the market power of core firms must diminish. New competition from outside core firms may well result in the restructuring of dominant firm relationships within an industry. However, such restructuring does not imply that a qualitatively different relationship will result between the surviving core firms or between such core firms and periphery firms.

Summary

The period of mergers, consolidations, and integration led to the establishment of groups of dominant core firms in some of the largest and fastest-growing manufacturing industries. It established a new structure of competition with sharp differentiation between core and periphery firms. Initially competition between core firms was largely restricted to intraindustry competition best characterized, despite many variations, as oligopolistic corespective behavior. Direct competition between core and periphery firms occurred primarily within core-dominated industries.

As core firms developed, structural constraints in their home industries dictated a new strategy for continued growth and profitability. Diversification allowed core firms to escape those constraints and gradually extend their market power outside their relatively narrow industrial bases. This strategy led to increased intracore competition in the new high-growth, advanced-technology areas.

The outcome of this industry-level dynamic was increasing aggregate domination of the economy by core firms. The proportion of total production controlled by core firms increased significantly, while membership in the core was extremely stable. This argument about the importance of aggregate concentration and firm size is in marked contrast to accepted wisdom within the field of industrial organization. Three well-known quotes serve as illustration of this wisdom. Morris Adelman opined that "absolute size is absolutely irrelevant";[98] George Stigler argued in a review of A.D.H. Kaplan's study of turnovers that "the statistical universe of the hundred or two hundred largest corporations is inappropriate to studies of monopoly and competition, and we may hope that this will be the last study to fall prey to its dramatic irrelevance";[99] and, finally, Jesse Markham has suggested that "In sum, 'market power' and 'bigness' are simply, like obesity and pregnancy, different conditions requiring different remedies."[100]

In each case the authors argued that the appropriate frame of reference for examining questions of monopoly, competition, or market power is the industry. Stigler, for example, continued, "For Kaplan's central idea—that the extent of in-

[98] Adelman 1965.
[99] Stigler 1956, p. 37.
[100] Markham 1965.

stability in the relative fortunes of leading firms is an inform-
ative symptom of competition—is important and deserves to
be applied on a correct industry basis."[101] This line of reasoning is fully consistent with the standard industrial organization
approach. However, the argument of this study is that the appropriate frame of reference for an analysis of competition can
never be a single industry but must include capital flows between industries. It is the importance of interindustry capital
mobility that makes relevant the study of that group of firms
in the economy distinguished by a combination of absolute
size and joint market share. A narrow focus on a market definition of competition treats every firm as if it resides in a single
market and ignores the phenomena of large firm size and diversification.

The logical distinction between size and market power made
by industrial organization authors is a correct one, as is the distinction between absolute and relative size. In the core–periphery view, size alone is not adequate to ensure membership in
the core. Size is a necessary but not sufficient condition for core
membership; joint market share is also required. There is a
substantial intersection, however, of the set of all core firms
and the set of the largest 100, 200, or 500 firms. Thus, studies
which employ aggregate concentration and other measures
based on those sets of large firms are relevant to hypotheses
about core firms. In a situation of extremely limited data, they
provide significant information beyond what can be provided
by analyses of individual industries. Together with data on
patterns of diversification, trends in industrial concentration,
and the stability of core membership, such studies provide support for the view that the core is a significant and substantial
part of the economy.

Although core firms may be eternal, that status is not maintained without an ongoing competitive struggle. Core firms'
record of stability and industry-specific and aggregate dominance did not result from a sleepy insouciance. Core firms have

---

[101] Stigler 1956, p. 37.

and will continue to compete vigorously. The historical evidence shows that core firms have actively pursued new industries and technologies via diversification and that core firms can be expected to continue to do so as the pace of technological change quickens. From a purely domestic perspective, U.S.-based core firms face serious new competition in many industries and new constraints on expansion as a result of intensified foreign competition. This is a significant event but not one that necessarily or even probably implies that the long-term result will be increased competition in the normative sense. Core firms have from the time of their formation and consolidation competed actively in international markets. Foreign firms are now confronting core firms in their U.S. markets. The core–periphery theory suggests that the ultimate result will be the emergence of a core group defined in terms of international markets and that current U.S. core firms will constitute a large proportion of that group.

Theories of Industry Structure and Competition

THE industrial organization literature implicitly and explicitly employs a theory of competition which is quite different from that advanced in chapter two. The much smaller body of work, here dubbed the dual economy literature, employs a variety of implicit and explicit approaches to competition which are, in turn, different in varying degrees from those presented in chapter two. This chapter reviews some of the salient aspects of the theories of competition in each literature and contrasts them with the core–periphery theory.

THE INDUSTRIAL ORGANIZATION TRADITION

The industrial organization tradition (hereafter the IO tradition) embodies a concept of competition that gives primary importance to individual industries. In this tradition, competition takes place within industries and industries are the main focus of attention. The trinity of the IO tradition, that is, structure, conduct, and performance, defines the framework for this intraindustry analysis of competition.[1]

The structure of an industry includes the number and size distribution of firms, the cost structures of firms, product characteristics, and demand characteristics. Industry structure is held to shape the conduct of firms in an industry. Conduct encompasses elements of firm behavior from pricing strategy to advertising to product differentiation to collusion. Finally,

[1] Several representative texts serve to make the point: Bain 1968; Caves 1972; Shepherd 1979; Scherer 1980.

structure, via its influence on conduct, produces a pattern of firm performance. The basic indicator of firm performance is the profit rate, which in turn is a key to broader measures of the performance of the economy like efficiency and the level of employment.[2]

The structure, conduct, and performance paradigm defines the important questions for the study of industrial organization within the IO tradition. These questions are almost solely concerned with an industry in isolation. The relevant structure is the internal structure of an industry. Conduct takes place within industries, and industry performance is the focus of interest, although it may also indicate something about the level of competitive forces in the broader economy.[3]

In the IO tradition, definitions of "perfect" or "industry" competition derived from general equilibrium theory include the condition that competition in the economy requires the free mobility of resources across industries. The conditions for perfect competition in the neoclassical analysis are that there be many profit-maximizing firms in each industry, homogeneous products within industries, full knowledge of market conditions, and free interindustry capital mobility.[4] However, industrial organization theorists have defined another concept, "pure" or "market" competition that takes place solely within an industry and for which the only condition is that there be many sellers. Thus, competition in a theoretically meaningful sense is held to be possible within an industry. It is this latter definition which actually informs analysis within the IO tradition.[5]

The IO tradition takes competition as its benchmark, but it does so in a restrictive fashion in that the only defining element of competition is an atomistically structured market. Given this limited definition, analysis can determine whether an in-

[2] Ibid.
[3] Ibid.
[4] Ferguson 1969.
[5] Bain 1956, pp. 1–4; Bain 1968, pp. 23–24; Scherer 1970, p. 10; Stigler 1957, p. 15; Stigler 1968, pp. 1–4.

dustry is competitive by a detailed examination of its structural characteristics. While the study of industrial organization has included a large proportion of industry case studies, broader cross-sectional studies also embody the single industry perspective.[6]

The strong concern with public policy that characterizes the IO tradition has strengthened the tendency to concentrate on single industries. The importance of competition and the conditions sufficient to ensure competition derive in large part from a concern with its opposites, oligopoly and monopoly, and the problems they pose for public policy. Competition has positive normative value in economic theory because under certain conditions competition will produce an efficient and optimal allocation of resources. Any deviation from competition implies a deviation from that standard. The IO tradition has focussed on the presence or absence of monopoly in individual industries precisely because the answer has implications for how well the economy as a whole is functioning, and thus for public policy toward those industries.[7]

In policy-oriented analysis the centrality of monopoly, which can be defined solely on an industry basis, leads to an analysis of the presence of varying degrees of monopoly and reduces competition to one end of the spectrum of monopoly market structures. As monopoly is legitimately defined on a single industry, a single industry becomes the appropriate framework for the general analysis of competition.

Workable Competition

The development of the concept of workable competition illustrates both the roots of the IO tradition in public policy concerns and its focus on single industries. The concept of workable competition was part of the earliest developments of the

[6] Bain 1956, pp. 1–4.

[7] For documentation that public policy concerns have shaped the analysis of industrial organization, see the texts cited in note 1. See also the "competition and monopoly" section in chapter three.

field and continues in various manifestations to have a significant role.[8] The rationale for workable competition was stated succinctly by Jesse Markham: "Economists, recognizing the shortcomings of the theory of perfect competition in framing public policy for oligopolistic markets, recently have endeavored to define a more realistic standard of economic performance—workable competition."[9] Stephen Sosnick presents a similar rationale in his encyclopedic review of the literature: "The theory of workable competition is best understood as an attempt to indicate what practically attainable states of affairs are socially desirable in individual capitalistic markets."[10]

In the theory of workable competition questions of generalized interindustry competition are shunted aside, as they are in the construct of "market" competition. Further, the theory of workable competition suggests that the intraindustry conditions consistent with perfect or even market competition are irrelevant. Sosnick argues, "the point is that the set of market structure and conduct attributes which define 'perfect competition' constitute individually and collectively neither a normative ideal nor a satisfactory basis for appraising actual market conditions."[11]

Public policy explicitly and exclusively provided the motivation for the theory of workable competition. The model of perfect competition was judged not useful in framing public policy for an economy comprised largely of industries that did not conform to the model, and it was even less useful in guiding the formation of policy toward individual oligopolistic industries. The requirements of a policy oriented toward individual industries led to a definition of competition designed to serve those needs rather than for its theoretical coherence.[12]

[8] J. M. Clark 1940; Markham 1950; Mason 1957; Sosnick 1958.
[9] Markham 1950.
[10] Sosnick 1958.
[11] Ibid.
[12] The concept of workable competition continues to have a public policy role. See, for example U.S. Federal Trade Commission 1980; U.S. Federal Trade Commission 1979.

Definitions of workable competition are an attempt to establish a set of standards for structure, conduct, and/or performance which guarantee "acceptable" social results. Rigid enforcement of the conditions required for perfect competition would be, it is argued, destructive and counterproductive in a modern industrial setting. A wide range of supportive arguments include references to the existence of economies of scale and the application of the theory of the second best.[13]

There were and are a variety of definitions of workable competition, in fact, nearly as many as authors on the topic. They have in common lists of structural attributes phrased in ambiguous terms: "There must be an appreciable number of sources of supply and an appreciable number of potential customers for substantially the same product or service";[14] "an industry is workably competitive when there are a considerable number of firms selling closely related products in each important product area."[15]

The theory of workable competition employs a "mixture of theory and ad hoc analysis" based on subjective notions of acceptable performance, structure, or conduct.[16] While this is not meant to suggest that workable competition is not a useful construct or that its basis in pragmatic policy concerns is invalid, it does provide, in admittedly extreme form, a useful illustration of the problem, from the viewpoint of the theory of core and periphery, with analysis in the 10 tradition. The theory of workable competition demonstrates the limits of an analysis which derives its basic structure from the policy problems of individual industries.

Although theories of workable competition are not homo-

---

[13] The reasoning is that insofar as there are deviations from competitive markets (for example, public utilities), it does not follow from general equilibrium theory that maintaining competition in the remaining markets has any necessary connection with optimality.

[14] C. Edwards 1949, p. 9.

[15] Stigler 1942, p. 2. Stigler also adds that 1) the firms not collude and 2) that there be no long-run cost disadvantage to new entrants.

[16] Markham 1950; Sosnick 1958; Stigler 1968.

geneous, well-articulated versions have used the same basic analytic approach, derived from the framework of the field of industrial organization, to establish criteria for workable competition in individual markets. There is another class of analyses within that framework which suggests how competitive forces may operate despite their apparent absence in the short run. These include theories of long-run competition, creative destruction, long-run substitution, potential competition, and contestable markets. Potential competition will be briefly analyzed as representative of this class in order to highlight further the differences in approach between the core–periphery analysis and that embodied in the industrial organization literature.

Potential Competition

Although analyses in the 10 tradition do not in general take explicit account of interindustry competition, there is a class of analyses which addresses at least part of that question, the impacts of potential entry on industry conduct and performance. The potential competition approach differs from that of workable competition in that it does not pose standards. It proposes a dynamic by which the results of active competition may be realized despite apparent deviations from the structural conditions of perfect competition. Theories of potential competition suggest that despite variations from competitive conditions, competition will probably be effective over time in most industries.

The basic notion of potential competition is that if firms with some advantage in an industry raise their prices and profits high enough, they will attract new entry, total production will expand, and profits will be reduced to the competitive level. As a result these firms may set their price below the short-run profit-maximizing level in order to maintain their market dominance.[17] The limit price model in its various permutations

17 Marshall 1970.

provides a detailed theory of pricing behavior by monopoly or oligopoly firms under the threat of potential entry.[18] Potential competition in general and the limit price model in particular are held to provide explanations of how even the profit rates of firms with substantial market power are limited by the force of competition. Further, in some interpretations the limit price model suggests that there is a dynamic at work in industries dominated by a few firms which not only limits their profit rates but also leads almost inevitably to an erosion of their position.

Entry will be attractive to some firms if they can earn "normal" profits and will be attractive to more firms if there is the promise of supranormal profits. The likelihood of profitable operations by a new entrant in an industry depends on its costs and on the price it will be able to charge. The size of this price–cost margin for a new entrant depends in turn on the structural conditions of entry and on the pricing behavior of established firms. The limit price is simply the highest price which established firms can charge without making it possible for a new entrant to earn at least a normal rate of profit.[19]

Existing firms must have specific advantages in order to earn above-normal profits without attracting entry. The "conditions of entry" into an industry are defined by the differences between the limit price and the "competitive" price. The conditions of entry, and thus the amount of above-normal profits, are determined by the presence or absence of barriers to entry, which encompass the range of advantages that existing firms may have over a potential entrant. Barriers to entry fall into three categories; product differentiation; absolute cost advantages, which include resource ownership, superior access to investible funds, and the requirement of a large absolute amount of capital in order to begin production; and economies of scale.[20]

[18] See for example: Bain 1956; Gaskins 1971; Modigliani 1958; Sylos-Labini 1969.
[19] Ibid.
[20] Bain 1956, pp. 4–25.

Industries can then be characterized according to their overall conditions of entry. Entry is blockaded in industries where the limit price is greater than the profit-maximizing price, that is potential competition has no effect on the profit rate. Entry is effectively impeded in industries where the limit price impedes entry and allows established firms to earn significant supranormal profits, although prices above the limit price will both increase short-run profits and induce entry. Entry is ineffectively impeded in industries where the limit price is below the short-run profit maximizing price and only slightly above the competitive price. Finally, entry is easy in industries where any price above the competitive price will induce entry, that is, where the limit price equals the competitive price.[21]

The effects of the overall conditions of entry into an industry are influenced by several additional factors. The degree of concentration and the resultant interdependence and ease of collusion will affect industry pricing policies and thus the level of profits earned as well as the amount of actual entry.[22] The source of the structural barriers to entry will also affect the amount and duration of any supranormal profits. In particular it is argued that *economies of scale* will have the most serious anticompetitive effects because they will result in high levels of concentration and will lead to a further increase in entry barriers as entry takes place.[23]

Observed profit rates will also depend on firms' pricing behavior. In the case of large-scale entry, it is the price likely to prevail after entry which determines what the entrant's profits will be, and thus the attractiveness of entry. The established firms may simply accede to new entry by cutting back output so that price remains at its pre-entry level or they may maintain output so that price falls and the new entrant has difficulty in earning even normal profits. The post-entry price is determined by the established firms' conduct which is in turn con-

[21] Ibid.
[22] Stigler 1970, pp. 20–23.
[23] Scherer 1970, pp. 244–45.

ditioned by the structural conditions which characterize the industry.[24]

Established firms may choose different pricing strategies under similar conditions of entry. A firm in an industry where entry is ineffectively impeded may choose to maximize short-run profits and lose market position, to limit price, or to price between the two so as to induce limited entry. The exact choice which a firm in such a situation makes depends in part on its attitude toward uncertainty and its time preferences. For example, if such a firm applies a high discount rate to profits earned in the future it will probably set its price above the limit price, thereby maximizing short-run profits while encouraging entry and eventual erosion of those profit levels.

The limit pricing model has two divergent implications for the interindustry structure of profit rates. The first is that the outcome will be a set of heterogeneous profit rates across industries with no apparent relation between them, and the second is that the outcome will be a single rate of profit across all industries.

The analysis which implies the first outcome emphasizes the importance of barriers to entry. Although the limit price model suggests the importance of dynamic capital flows, barriers are treated as part of an industry's structure in the same way that concentration or the size distribution of firms is treated in the IO tradition. Rather than serving to introduce interindustry capital mobility, barriers to entry are seen only within a framework of single industries, where each industry has a particular set of barriers which impede entry in varying degrees.[25] Barriers to entry contribute to an explanation of above-average profit rates in particular industries, but they do not contribute to an explanation of how that average rate of profit is formed or determined.

This analysis emphasizes the impediments to capital flows to the exclusion of potential sources of these capital flows which

[24] Sylos-Labini 1969.
[25] Bain 1956, p. 3.

could result in variation in the intensity of competition or likelihood of entry. It ignores the problem of a firm's reinvestment decision in an industry protected by barriers and fails to specify what, if any, limitations exist to the rate of profit of such firms apart from the threat of entry. Since Joe Bain and others have suggested that the limit price model is relevant to a substantial number of major industries in the economy, this question is of some importance. The emphasis on heterogeneity of industries which is the outcome of this industry by industry approach means that each industry has a peculiar set of entry conditions. The result is a heterogeneous set of supranormal profit rates against a background of normal profit rates prevailing in most industries.

The analysis which implies a homogeneous profit rate across industries suggests that for above-average profits to persist despite potential entry, substantial barriers to entry must exist together with high levels of concentration, that is, entry must be blockaded or effectively impeded. F. M. Scherer argues that these conditions "appear to be more the exception than the rule," and that the most important barrier to entry, economies of scale over the whole range of output, exists only rarely, while flat long-run average cost curves are typical in U.S. industry.[26] Scherer argues that because the conditions required for persistent above-average profits do not exist to a significant degree, the worst case postulated by the limit price model does not pose a serious threat to competition. Scherer states, ". . . the prevalent case is one in which unit production and distribution costs are roughly constant once a minimum optimal scale considerably smaller than the market size is attained. This evidence, coupled with predictions generated by the theory, suggests that the market shares of dominant firms will commonly display a declining trend."[27] In addition, other barriers like product differentiation are not, in this view, adequate to create widespread supranormal profits.

[26] Scherer 1980, p. 252.
[27] Scherer 1970, pp. 216–31; see also Worcester 1957.

The outcome in this second analysis appears to be a tendency toward the "normal" rate of profit across all industries. From this perspective, the limit price model provides a view of dominant firms and groups of firms in which they tend never to be faced with the problem of reinvesting their profits. Although some firms may maintain supranormal profits over an extended period as a result of an advantageous set of entry barriers, in general dominant firms or groups of firms are squeezed by new entrants or the threat of new entrants to the point where profits are close to "normal" and apparently just sufficient for internal reinvestment or are such that these firms are actually squeezed out of the market. In the long run, industry profit rates will probably tend toward a single rate, although it is never clearly specified that this is the expected result.

A new and more fully developed theory which may be appropriately dealt with under the general heading of potential competition, although it represents an extension and a systematization of the theory, is that of contestable markets. The essential conclusion of the contestable markets analysis is that under conditions of "absolutely free entry" and "absolutely costless exit," that is, contestability, an industry will display all the welfare attributes of perfect competition regardless of the internal structure of the industry, given that there are at least two firms. That potential entrants can thus reap any above-normal profits via short-term "hit and run" entry and exit suffices to maintain industry profits at normal levels. This potential entry is assumed to be at a scale consistent with that of dominant firms and to take place quickly, without significant retaliation. The result here is also a tendency toward a normal rate of profit across all industries.[28]

The limitations of the industrial organization paradigm are reflected in the analyses of potential competition as well as in the analysis of workable competition. Despite divergent outcomes, the analyses of potential competition treat the individ-

[28] For a summary see Baumol 1982.

ual industry as the locus of competition. The potential competition analyses do move one step beyond the purely
intraindustry analysis typified by workable competition, but
remain focussed on individual industries in isolation. After assuming that real potential entrants exist for any industry, it
follows that "competitive" results are more likely within an industry regardless of whether actual entry takes place.

That potential entrants are simply assumed to exist both illustrates this narrow focus and constitutes the limitation of the
potential competition analysis. An explanation of the sources
of new capital for entry is essential to a full theory of competition. In the neoclassical model, capital is completely mobile
and can shift between industries in response to profit differentials. In the world of real firms, which have their capital tied up
in physical assets and where there are barriers to entry, the
source of new entry is not as clear, particularly since the potential competition model itself implies internal constraints on the
capital available even for large firms in concentrated industries. Their profits are limited by an intraindustry dynamic. In
the extreme case their profits and market share are shrinking
in the industry they "dominate." Under such pressure these
firms are in no position to invest outside the industry where
such investment would mean entering a new market. If this is
the case for large profitable firms, it must also be true for
smaller firms which face even more severe constraints than do
the large firms. In short, the potential competition model provides no systematic explanation of the sources of the new investment that is held to have such beneficial effects. This is an
especially important omission given the quantities of investment capital required to provide real competition for large
firms in concentrated industries.

In contrast with earlier variants of the potential competition
approach, the contestable markets analysis does provide an
explanation of the source of new capital by returning to the neoclassical assumption that exit is costless; a firm may simply
sell off its assets in its old industry and without the hindrance
of barriers to entry enter a more profitable industry at the ap-

propriate scale. The contestable markets approach is a complete theory of competition which explains on an inter- and intraindustry basis how, subject to certain restrictive assumptions, desired performance goals may emerge despite industry structures normally associated with noncompetitive outcomes.[29] The difficulty with this approach is that the assumptions, like those of the perfectly competitive model, are not very plausible when analyzing competition in the current institutional context, which is the difficult task approached by other industrial organization analysts.

In sum, analysis in the IO tradition has in general focussed narrowly upon individual industries rather than on the interindustry requirements for competition. Concurrently, the analysis has tended to support the belief that competition is adequate in the U.S. economy. That these analytical examples represent a broader trend is supported by William Shepherd, who concluded that a growing consensus of expert opinion was, among other things, that "the natural structure and behavior of most markets are now commonly thought to be competitive in essential respects."[30] However, this consensus is based upon a generally incomplete theory of competition, which has been applied in an ad hoc manner exemplified by both workable and potential competition. Consistent with the trend is the "Chicago school" attack on the consensus interpretation of the empirical results on the relation between concentration and profitability. This body of literature provides further illustration of the themes delineated in this chapter and is addressed explicitly in chapter five.

THE DUAL ECONOMY LITERATURE

A relatively small number of authors have explicitly addressed the existence of a core and periphery, by whatever name, and the implications of that existence for the economic perform-

---

[29] For a critique of the contestable markets approach, see Shepherd 1984.
[30] Shepherd 1970; Shepherd 1982; Scherer 1980.

ance of firms and of the economy. A more or less comprehensive list must include Robert Averitt, Paul Baran, Alfred Chandler, Richard Edwards, Alfred Eichner, John Kenneth Galbraith, James O'Connor, Gerry Oster, Howard Sherman, Josef Steindl, Paul Sweezy, and Harold Vatter.[31] Though only the work of Averitt and Sweezy will be reviewed in detail, a few general comments about this literature help to place it in the perspective of this study. References in the text and footnotes demonstrate for the others my dependence on or differences with their analyses.

The dual economy approach in its broadest sense, which means only recognition of qualitative differences between core and periphery groups, has been used to make arguments about a variety of topics. They range from the implications of a core–periphery industrial structure for macroeconomic performance[32] to firm-specific performance and public policy implications[33] to the structure of labor markets, which derives from the underlying industrial structure.[34] While there is agreement on the broad structure of competition, there is systematic disagreement on most other important areas of the argument. Firm goals are held to range from profit maximization to sales maximization to some combination, while the dynamic underlying the dual firm/industrial structure is held to vary from large firm attempts to establish market power in the pursuit of long-run profits to a technological imperative that leads to the establishment of large firms whose market power is required by modern industrial technology.[35]

A fundamental disagreement in this literature centers on

[31] Averitt 1968; Baran and Sweezy 1966; Chandler 1959; 1969; R. Edwards 1979; Eichner 1976; Galbraith 1967; O'Connor 1973; Sherman 1968; Steindl 1945; 1952; Sweezy 1942; Vatter 1975. It should be noted that this list does not include those who primarily analyze segmented labor markets.

[32] Eichner 1976; Steindl 1952.

[33] Averitt 1968.

[34] See for example: Bluestone 1970; Buchele 1976; Cain 1976; Doeringer and Piore 1971; Gordon, Edwards, and Reich 1982.

[35] See note 31.

whether the appropriate unit of analysis is the firm or the industry. When the industry is the unit of analysis, the economy is divided into core and periphery industries which are characterized as homogeneous entities with clear sets of attributes. James O'Connor, for example, states: "Production and distribution in the private sector fall into two subgroups: competitive industries organized by small business and monopolistic industries organized by large-scale capital."[36] Gerry Oster, in an article that provided one of the first empirical tests of the dual economy theory, characterized that theory as suggesting a U.S. economy "composed of two distinct industrial groups: a core of powerful, concentrated, unionized, capital-intensive, technologically progressive industries, and a periphery composed of industries marked by the absence of these features."[37]

Others within the dual economy literature employ the firm as the unit of analysis. Averitt, Edwards, Galbraith, and Steindl, for example, each focus on the attributes of individual firms as central to definitions of core and periphery membership. The present study also takes the firm as the unit of analysis. Such an approach recognizes that core and periphery firms with significantly different structural, behavioral, and performance characteristics may coexist within an industry and that while some industries may be composed of relatively homogeneous firms, many are not. Firms are the actors within an economy structured by industries. While there are significant interactions between firm and industry characteristics only an analysis of firms and industries as distinct entities permits an understanding of those interactions.

The industry focus makes analysis of performance both conceptually and empirically difficult. Oster's separation of industries into core and periphery via a factor analysis, which separates the sectors primarily via industry size variables and the level of concentration, does not find a significant loading on the profit rate variable. No direct measures of risk were used.

[36] O'Connor 1973, p. 13.
[37] Oster 1978, p. 33.

The same problem arises in the industrial organization literature when industry profit rates are used as a measure of performance. (See chapter five.) The factor analysis approach to specifying core and periphery industries also confuses current attributes of core-dominated industries, for example, capital intensity, with conceptually necessary attributes of core-dominated industries. As manufacturing plays a smaller role in aggregate economic activity, core firms can be expected to shift into and eventually dominate industries, various service industries, for example, which are not necessarily capital intensive.

The existence of large corporations has played a critical role in theories of segmented labor markets in that it is held to be the market power of such firms that creates the possibility for significantly different types of labor markets. However, much of the dual or segmented labor market empirical literature relies on a distinction between primary and secondary labor markets based on core and periphery industries rather than firms.[38] Some segmented labor market analyses explicitly note that while the firm is the appropriate unit of analysis, data limitations require the use of industry-based definitions of core and periphery sectors.[39] While the segmented labor market theory has become more sophisticated in that it recognizes different labor markets within as well as between firms, the underlying industrial structure analysis has not developed in a parallel fashion. This lack of development derives in large part from the primary use of the core–periphery distinction as a sorting device necessary to an analysis of labor markets rather than as a way of understanding competition.

Robert Averitt's *The Dual Economy* (1968) is a complete, consistent view of an economy bifurcated into center and periphery along firm lines. Firms are center firms by reason primarily of absolute size, and as a result of their behavior by reason of market power, vertical integration, and diversification.

[38] See note 34.
[39] Gordon, Edwards, and Reich 1982, pp. 192–93.

Center firms, because of their size and structure, are virtually eternal, as long as management steers a steady course.

Averitt presents his analysis as a new approach to the theory of the firm and criticizes the long-run neoclassical theory of the firm and in particular its lack of a convincing reason why a firm's long-run average cost curve should turn up at some point.[40] He argues that a two-part theory should replace the neoclassical theory. Periphery firms can be fairly represented as typical neoclassical firms. Their long-run cost curves turn up for reasons which derive from their competitive position vis-à-vis center firms. After a certain amount of expansion, periphery firms face constraints from technologically inferior equipment and inelastic factor supply curves, primarily those for credit and managerial talent. Their size and market position limit their internal resources and limit their access to high-quality outside resources.[41]

Center firms, on the other hand, possess downward sloping or at least flat long-run cost curves. They face no absolute limits to size, although their growth rate may be constrained. Their size and profits make it possible to build new plants rather than to strain old ones and their backward integration makes it possible to obtain unlimited quantities of inputs without forcing up the price. Their size and profits also mean that they have access to both internally generated and borrowed capital and that they have high-quality management, the most important factors of production in Averitt's view.[42]

While the theory of competition associated with this theory of the firm is not as clearly delineated, the structure of intraindustry competition is clear. In some cases, core and periphery firms coexist, while in others only periphery firms exist. There are no important cases where core firms exist without periphery firms in an industry. Averitt has an elaborate taxonomy of center–periphery structural relations. Periphery firms may be

[40] Averitt, pp. 84–86.
[41] Ibid., pp. 86–94.
[42] Ibid., pp. 105–128.

satellites, loyal opposition, or free agents: Satellites have either forward or backward vertical linkages to center firms and they may or may not be formally in the same industry with those center firms; loyal opposition firms are periphery firms operating within the home industry of center firms; free agents are the remaining periphery firms and include those which operate in periphery-dominated industries as well as in niches in center-dominated industries.[43]

Averitt does not present the goals of the firm as clearly as he does the structure of competition. While periphery firms are characterized as close to the firm of microeconomics textbooks, their goals are not specified. It is not clear, for example, whether they are profit-maximizers, satisficers, or growth maximizers. Their goals vary: Some periphery firms simply "follow conventional periphery management techniques: they rely on tested methods of producing and distribute long-accepted products"; others aspire to membership in the center; and still others pioneer new products or processes in the hopes of a "financial windfall."[44]

A similar lack of specificity obtains in Averitt's discussion of center firm goals. It is clear that center firms are not short-run profit maximizers; their outlook is long run. Averitt argues that center firms "do not maximize short-run profits as oligopoly theory predicts, for to do so would invite poor public relations and endanger long-run survival."[45] As a result he seems to adopt the sales maximization hypothesis without considering the alternative, equally consistent with his evidence, long-run profit maximization. Averitt frequently asserts that sales growth is the basic strategy with which center firms meet all threats, for example, "The first rule of survival in any but the worst times is not cut expenses, but expand sales."[46] Further, ". . . there is evidence that many center firms seek to maximize sales revenue subject to a profit restraint."[47] He sug-

[43] Ibid., pp. 86–104.
[44] Ibid.
[45] Ibid., p. 113.
[46] Ibid., p. 18.
[47] Ibid., p. 113.

gests at the same time, however, that a high growth rate of assets and the attainment of "economic size" are important center firm characteristics.[48] He argues that size is the key characteristic of center firms but never specifies the relevant measure of size or how the size measure derives from the firm's goals.

In the context of pricing policies, Averitt argues that center firms probably have a variety of goals. "Perhaps all three theories of pricing practice—short-run profit maximization, cost-plus markups, and sales maximization with a minimum profit restraint—are correct."[49] The specific pricing strategy chosen is held to be a function of the production type. Averitt does suggest, in the case of pricing strategy for firms with mass-produced output, that some form of oligopolistic pricing might be consistent with maximizing long-run profits. "One might argue that survival pricing maximizes very long-run profit during the lifetime of participating firms, but it does not result in the necessary equation of short-run marginal cost and revenue."[50] Averitt confuses the conditions for short-run profit maximization with those for long-run profit maximization. Again, he fails to specify clearly long-run profit maximization as an alternative firm goal and fails to consider that all the observed forms of pricing behavior are potentially consistent with long-run profit maximization. As a result, his arguments for sales maximization are not persuasive and his measures of center performance are imprecise. The argument that expansion is "the first rule of survival" does not imply that this expansion is of sales with a profit constraint rather than an expansion of assets, driven by profit maximization. Neither does the fact that successful center firms must be dynamic, responsive, and long-run oriented imply that they must be sales rather than profit maximizers. The point is that Averitt's characterization of firms as, for example, expansionist or technologically

[48] Ibid., pp. 19, 101.
[49] Ibid., p. 30.
[50] Ibid., p. 31.

dynamic, does not distinguish between the two hypotheses about their goals.

Averitt's ambiguity about firm goals is carried over into his discussion of interindustry capital flows. While Averitt never explicitly characterizes center firm diversification as interindustry capital flows, that is the role it serves within his theory of competition. For Averitt, diversification is the key to center firm immortality; when the expansion of old markets slows, center firms can diversify into more attractive areas. Expansive center firms must diversify out of slow-growth markets into new fast-growing markets characterized by technological innovation; the imperative is sales growth to overcome technological obsolescence.[51]

However, Averitt's theoretical explanation of why center firms diversify hints at profit-maximizing rather than sales-maximizing behavior. Averitt argues that center firms diversify in order to maintain long-run marginal revenue. Further, they attempt to create the largest possible distance between their gradually declining long-run average cost curves and their "average marginal revenue" curve.[52] Again, Averitt advances conflicting hypotheses about firm goals and thus the incentive for diversification.

This ambiguity about firm goals and thus about interindustry capital mobility leaves Averitt without a clear measure with which to evaluate the outcome of competition. Averitt ignores the question of profit rates and implicitly denies that the process of core and periphery competition will lead to the formation of two rates of profit. Rather, corporate profits and assets are "unevenly distributed" between center and periphery, while profit rates are never explicitly discussed. Instead, center firms have "large cash flows" while a periphery firm's "cash flow is smaller"; or center firms have "abundant financial resources" while periphery firms have "poorer credit ratings." Center firms are generally characterized as "expansive" rather

[51] Ibid., pp. 14–20.
[52] Ibid., p. 110.

than profitable.[53] The outcome of Averitt's competition is really structural: the center and periphery reproduce themselves. Center firms expand and have adequate resources while periphery firms stagger along without those resources.

Paul Sweezy presents a model of an economy in which industries are divided into monopoly and competitive sectors.[54] The monopoly sector comprises industries dominated by monopolists or small groups of "monopolists" and the remaining industries form a "hierarchy" of structures ranging down to highly competitive.[55] This structure, which is the result of a historical process of concentration and centralization of capital, disrupts the tendency toward an equal interindustry rate of profit that prevailed under the earlier, more competitive regime. Large monopoly firms, operating behind impermeable barriers to entry in monopoly industries, earn high profits while smaller firms ensconced in competitive industries earn low profits. According to Sweezy, the initial result of this structure of competition is a hierarchy of profit rates corresponding to the hierarchy of industry structures, while the longer-run tendency is toward an increased bifurcation of industry profit rates. This "intensification of distortions in the pattern of profit rates which monopoly originally brings with it" seems to imply that the hierarchy of profit rates is reduced to two profit rates, one in monopoly industries and one in competitive industries.

However, the process by which this increased bifurcation takes place is spelled out in a contradictory manner; it leads analytically to a single, low rate of profit rather than two distinct rates. Sweezy's analysis of a monopoly firm's investment decision suggests that the alternatives are to reinvest in its

[53] Ibid., p. 2.

[54] Sweezy 1942.

[55] The model discussed here is drawn from the two chapters on monopoly in Sweezy 1942, "The Development of Monopoly Capital" and "Monopoly and the Laws of Motion of Capitalism." Sweezy's second book, *Monopoly Capital*, does not address the interaction between the monopoly and competitive sectors.

home industry or to invest in a competitive industry, assuming that barriers to entry preclude investment in another monopoly industry. In examining this choice, Sweezy says; "We observe the following apparent paradox, namely that a monopolist making large profits will nevertheless refuse to invest more capital in his own industry and will search for outside opportunities for investment even though the rate of profit obtainable be much lower." The paradox disappears when analysis shows that the investment decision depends on the "marginal profit rate," which is "the rate on the additional investment after allowance has been made for the fact that the additional investment, since it will increase output and reduce price, will entail a reduction in profit on the old investment."

Sweezy's apparent paradox and subsequent resolution derive from the neoclassical analysis of monopoly firms. With a given industry demand curve, a profit-maximizing monopolist will produce up to but not including the point where marginal revenue is zero and demand elasticity is unitary. The exact point of production chosen depends on the location of the cost curves. To produce beyond that profit-maximizing point implies that total revenue must fall and that the rate of profit on fixed investment in plant and equipment must also fall. It is worth noting that Sweezy's definition of marginal profit rate places the monopoly firm at its profit-maximizing output. Only if the firm produces beyond that point will a "reduction in profit on the old investment" be entailed.[56]

[56] Sweezy's example places the monopolist firm at the point on its demand curve where marginal revenue equals zero, while asserting that it still earns monopoly profits. Clearly, maximum profits occur at a much smaller level of output unless marginal cost is zero, which is not true in his example. If the firm were actually at this point, additional output must by definition earn negative marginal revenue.

The profit maximization point and the marginal-revenue-equals-zero point could also coincide in the case of an oligopoly firm facing a kinked demand curve where the undefined portion of the marginal revenue curve intersected the x-axis. However, Sweezy makes no reference to this possibility and its existence does not alter the analysis.

A possible additional explanation for operating at or above the output level

Sweezy's point, however, is to expand the static monopoly model. If a monopolist continues to invest its profits and expand output in its own industry it will eventually reach the point where its profits decline as a result. A monopolist's alternative is to invest elsewhere; for example, in a competitive industry where a positive profit can be earned on the investment without an impact on profits earned in the home industry. The monopolist will invest in a competitive industry if the marginal profit rate there is greater than the marginal profit rate on reinvestment in the home industry. In other words, monopolists will maximize their rate of profit on all invested capital, whether it is in the home industry or a competitive industry, by maximizing the profit rate on new investment while taking into account its potential effect in the home industry.

Sweezy argues that the result of this process of outside investment by monopoly firms is to drive down the profit rates in competitive industries while maintaining high profits in monopoly industries. The entrance of monopoly firms into competitive industries intensifies the level of competition and drives profits down there, while leaving intact the profits earned in the monopolized industry. While the analysis may hold to some extent at the industry level, that is, the profit rates earned in each type of industry may remain different, it clearly does not hold for firms. In fact, the investment dynamic described will have the opposite effect on firm profit rates; it will tend to equalize the profit rates of monopoly and competitive firms.

Firm profit rates would tend toward equality as monopoly firms pursue low-profit investments in competitive industries for the following reasons. A monopoly firm will reinvest profits in its own industry until the marginal profit rate in a competitive industry is higher. Investment in the competitive sector may drive down the industry profit rate there and make some subsequent investment in the monopoly industry attractive

where marginal revenue equals zero might be that the monopolist is engaged in limit pricing to inhibit entry. Sweezy makes no mention of this possibility.

again. In any case the rate of profit earned on these investments regardless of sector will be the rate which prevails in the competitive sector. The monopolist will not invest in a competitive industry until the average firm profit rate which results is higher than the average firm profit rate which would result from an investment in the home industry. In Sweezy's example, regardless of where the new investment is made, its result will be to lower the firm's average rate of profit, with the limit being the profit rate earned in the competitive industries. New investments and their lower profit rates will tend to bring the average firm rate of profit down to the level prevailing in the competitive sector. Thus, one lower firm profit rate emerges and it is determined in the limit by conditions prevailing in the competitive sector.

While some significant difference may remain between the profit rate earned by a monopoly firm in its home industry and that earned in the competitive sector, this divergence between industry profit rates will also be decreased by Sweezy's investment dynamic. Although low marginal profit rates coexist with high average profit rates for monopoly firms confined to their home industries, Sweezy's scenario does not provide any high marginal profit investment alternatives. As increased investment in the competitive sector drives down profit rates earned there; reinvestment in the home industry will bring down the monopoly industry average rate of return. The lower limit to which profit rates available in the competitive sector may decline determines the extent to which further investment in the monopoly industry takes place, and thus the degree to which the average monopoly industry profit rate converges with the competitive industry rate. Some convergence will certainly take place.

Rather than providing an explanation for continued centralization of capital under the control of monopoly firms, Sweezy's model implies that once monopoly firms move beyond the uniquely advantageous confines of their home industry they are reduced to equality with small competitive firms. The model fails for several reasons. The first is a confusion between industry and firm profit rates. Sweezy's discussion fails to distinguish monopoly firm from monopoly industry rate of profit and thus fails to establish the relationship between a monopoly firm's rate of profit and its investments in competitive industries. It is as a result of the failure to specify clearly such a relationship that the predicted intensification of the distortion in profit rates does not occur in the model.

The second reason, closely related to the first, is that while Sweezy's model is impeccably logical as far as it goes, it ignores a critical aspect of core firm investment behavior as it applies to investment in periphery industries. In recent history such investment has taken the form of diversification but core firm diversification does not proceed in such a way as to make a competitive industry more competitive. In fact, the effect, if diversification is successful, is to bring the industry under core firm domination. The core firm eventually realizes a high profit rate there, so that rather than bringing down the average firm profit rate the effect of outside investment is to bolster the firm's rate of profit and to allow continued profitable growth outside the confines of its home industry.

CHAPTER FIVE

Empirical Propositions on Industry Structure and Performance

THIS chapter will review selected portions of the industrial organization literature in order to specify the context for the hypotheses pertaining to core and periphery that were presented in chapter two and that will be tested in detail in chapter six. This chapter covers the following topics: (1) the relation between firm size and profitability; (2) the relation between firm and/or industry profitability and industry concentration levels; (3) the more complex relations among firm/industry profitability, absolute firm size, and industry concentration; (4) the relations among firm/industry profitability, absolute firm size, relative firm size, or market share, and industry concentration; (5) a summary of the market structure literature and its implications for the theory of core and periphery; (6) the relation between firm characteristics and various measures of risk.

SIZE AND PROFITABILITY

The core–periphery formulation suggests that large firms should generally have higher profit rates than small firms where size is measured across all firms in the economy or, more precisely, across all firms in the manufacturing sector. Insofar as core firms dominate the population of large firms there should be a positive bivariate relation between size and profitability.

The literature on the simple relationship between absolute firm size and rate of profit provides relatively consistent results.[1] They are that, subject to various qualifications, there is a positive nonlinear relation between size and profitability. The shape of the relationship is sensitive to assumptions about three exogenous variables: the time period chosen; the exclusion of corporations with negative profits; and adjustments for executive compensation.

A finding common to all the studies is that the shape of the size distribution of rates of return is reversed by the exclusion of firms that did not earn positive profits in any year. Among profitable firms, small firms earned slightly higher rates of return than large firms.[2] However, when all firms are included, the strong positive relation between rates of loss and size overwhelms that weaker negative correlation.[3] Clearly, the dispersion of profit rates for small firms is substantially greater than for large firms (see "Risk" section below). The fact that many small firms did not earn positive profits in any year provides important information about their competitive position and does not constitute a basis for omitting negative income firms from the analysis of size and profitability.

Most of the studies which focus primarily on the size–profitability relationship have analyzed IRS size class data for different portions of the 1930 to 1965 period.[4] The shape and in some cases the slope of the size–profitability relation show a marked pattern of variation with the exact period. Richard Osborn has shown that the shape of the relation varies with economic conditions, becoming flatter in periods of expansion and more positively sloped in periods of decline.[5] Howard Sherman, in addition, showed that the economic pressures associated with the war years exacerbated this normal cyclical relation and in some years dramatically changed the shape of

[1] Alexander 1949; Crum 1939; McConnell 1945; Osborn 1950; Sherman 1968; Stekler 1964; Stigler 1963.

[2] See, for example, Stekler 1963, p. 68.

[3] Ibid., small deficit firms have smaller (more negative) profit rates than do large deficit firms.

[4] See note 1.

[5] Osborn 1950, pp. 75–78.

the relationship.[6] However, analysis of the peacetime years between 1931 and 1961 shows a positive relation on average. Profitability rises steadily with asset size until the $10 to $50 million asset category where it levels off. The wartime years show a parabolic relation that rises, peaks between $0.5 and $50 million, and then declines slightly.[7]

It has been argued that small firms have an incentive to pay some of their profits to their officers as executive compensation in order to reduce the firms' tax exposure.[8] Since small corporations are frequently wholly owned by one or several officers, there is no outside stockholder pressure to limit compensation. As a result, it is argued that the profits of small corporations are understated and must be adjusted in some fashion before the true relation between size and profitability can be determined.

Two major classes of adjustments have been made with broadly similar results. Joseph McConnell's adjustment was based on the earnings of officers in a sample of firms with dispersed stock ownership.[9] Significant adjustments were limited to firms with less than $250,000 in assets in the 1939 to 1941 period. The adjustments generally more than doubled the calculated profit rates for these small firms, while the effect in firms with between $250,000 and $1 million in assets was minor. Overall, the shape of the size–profitability relation was not significantly changed although it was less steep for the smallest corporations.

Sidney Alexander adjusted the earnings of profitable small firms on the assumption that the earnings of executives in nonprofitable small firms represented the real "market value" of executives in such firms. Any compensation over those levels was considered true profit and added to the profit total for the affected size class. This type of adjustment (Stekler also used it)

---

[6] Sherman 1968.

[7] Ibid.

[8] Alexander 1949, pp. 233–35; Crum 1939, p. 310; McConnell 1945, p. 7; Stekler 1963, pp. 18–25; Stigler 1963, pp. 69–70.

[9] McConnell 1945.

had a larger effect than McConnell's adjustment but again did not significantly change the shape of the size–profitability relation.[10]

There is no direct evidence that the suggested bias in non-adjusted profit rates exists. In addition the logic of the argument is not overwhelming. Alexander's adjustment hypothesis ignores the incentive of officer-owners in unprofitable corporations to cut their own salaries in order to reduce firm losses and thus improve their position in financial markets. Further, it is not clear whether dispersed ownership increases or decreases the power of corporate officers despite McConnell's assumption that such power and dispersion are inversely related.

The adjustment hypothesis also assumes that there are no differences between executives, and that all interfirm profitability differences must result from the productivity of capital and production labor.[11] This problem in turn is related to the conceptual difficulty of distinguishing between the payment of wages for work performed by executives and the distribution of profits. McConnell's adjustment assumes that more than half of executive compensation in affected small firms is profit rather than wages.[12] Given that the average compensation in the years analyzed for officers in the smallest size class was about $1,500,[13] and that the average wage in manufacturing was $1,216,[14] this seems unlikely.

If the "profits" that are distributed as executive compensation are not reinvested but are simply excess costs, in order to properly evaluate the size–profitability relationship it would be necessary to evaluate the costs paid by firms of different sizes. It is frequently argued that large dominant firms do not have the same efficiency incentives as small firms and therefore

[10] Alexander 1949.
[11] Stigler 1963 makes this argument.
[12] McConnell 1945.
[13] Crum 1939, p. 314.
[14] U.S. Bureau of the Census 1965, ser. D739–64, p. 166.

pay more than "cost" for many items.[15] These excess costs are conceptually similar to excess executive compensation and provide a reverse bias to the data on size and profitability.

Finally, the adjustment techniques ignore other systematic forces which shape firm profitability and executive compensation. Dispersed stock ownership could reflect a weak financial position vis-à-vis closely held small corporations, which did not need to go to the stock market for funds.[16] This financial weakness may depress officer's salaries below their market value and thus bias upward the adjustments made by McConnell.

In any case the debate over appropriate adjustment of small firm profit rates is not directly relevant to the present study. The small firms included here range in size from $5 to $25 million in assets. IRS data indicate that only 0.3 percent of firms in these size classes in 1969 had limited or nondispersed stock ownership.[17] The firms analyzed in this study are all publicly held. Thus even if adjustments were justified they would have an imperceptible effect on the results of this study.

CONCENTRATION AND PROFITABILITY

The extant, plausible theories of oligopoly tend to suggest an inverse relation between the number of firms in an industry and the price level. This is in turn consistent with a positive relation between profitability and the level of concentration.[18] The presumed dynamic by which the existence of a small number of firms is translated into higher prices, and therefore profits, varies from the implausible behavioral assumptions of the Cournot or Bertrand models to the loosely specified modified-Chamberlin model, which seems to be widely accepted among empirically-minded industrial organization economists.[19] The

[15] The classic work in this area is Leibenstein 1966.
[16] Steindl 1945.
[17] U.S. Internal Revenue Service 1973, Table 22, p. 159.
[18] Scherer 1980, pp. 152–60.
[19] Ibid., Weiss 1974, pp. 185–93.

modified-Chamberlin model assumes that oligopolists recognize their mutual dependence and act cooperatively via mechanisms like collusion or price leadership to jointly maximize their rates of profit. The success with which such coordination is pursued depends on the underlying structural conditions, which include most importantly the homogeneity of firms' cost structures, firms' perceived price elasticities, the exact number and size structure of firms in the industry, the height of barriers to entry, and general industry conditions, especially the growth rate of demand.

On this basis the traditional hypothesis in industrial organization studies has been that high levels of concentration are associated with conditions necessary for successful collusion. This collusion results in above-average profit rates for firms in the industry and thus a positive association between industry profit rates and concentration.[20] The results of the empirical literature are generally quite consistent. Exhaustive reviews of the extensive literature on concentration and profitability by Leonard Weiss and others have concluded that there is a robust positive relation between concentration and industry profitability which persists over a variety of samples, measurement techniques, and time periods.[21]

A full review of the many studies will not be attempted here, as it has been performed thoroughly by several authors. Rather, a brief review of several paradigmatic studies is presented in order to clarify the basic results and the issues raised by them. The typical study in what will be termed the consensus literature tests a relationship in which the profit rate is functionally dependent upon concentration and some combination of variables which represent entry barriers and industry demand conditions.

Joe Bain's 1956 study provides the first illustration of an empirical test of the basic concentration–profitability model with barriers to entry taken into account. A cross-tabulation of in-

[20] Weiss 1974.
[21] Intriligator et al. 1973; Weiss 1971; Weiss 1974.

dustry profit rates for forty-two selected industries with levels
of concentration and estimates of barriers to entry for the periods 1936–1940 and 1948–1951 showed a positive impact
for both independent variables. Michael Mann extended the
analysis to include the 1950–1960 period and found similar effects.[22]

In a large-scale statistical investigation, Norman Collins and
Lee Preston analyzed the relation of industry price–cost margins to four-firm concentration ratios, and other variables at
the four-digit industry level.[23] They found overall a positive
significant relation. The following is a representative regression presented in their study:

$$\text{PCM} = 19.54 + 0.96 \text{ CONC} - .029 \text{ GD} + .092 \text{ KO}$$

where $N = 417$ industries, $R^2 = 0.19$, and the concentration
(CONC) coefficient was reported to be significant at the 1 percent level while the coefficients of geographic dispersion (GD)
and the capital-output ratio (KO) were significant at the 5 percent level. (The standard errors of the coefficients were not reported.)

Weiss analyzed the same relation of price–cost margin to
level of concentration with additional independent variables.[24]
His results were consistent with those of Collins and Preston.
Weiss estimated the following regression:

$$\text{PCM} = 16.3 + .050 \text{ CONC} - .029 \text{ GD} + .119 \text{ KO} +$$
$$(.024) \qquad (.010) \qquad (.016)$$

$$1.30 \text{ ADVT} - 1.9 \text{ CEMP} + .023 \text{ INV} + .26 \text{ GR}$$
$$(.18) \qquad (4.2) \qquad (.136) \qquad (.09)$$

$$+ .00083 \text{ CONC CDR} + .095 \text{ MID} - .033 \text{ PLTS}$$
$$(.00030) \qquad (.130) \qquad (.020)$$

with $N = 399$, $R^2 = .427$. Concentration had a significant positive effect on price–cost margins, which was more positive as

[22] Bain 1956; Mann 1966.
[23] Collins and Preston 1969, pp. 271–86.
[24] Weiss 1974; revised coefficients as reported in Scherer 1980.

the product of the concentration ratio and the proportion of consumer sales of total industry sales (CONC CDR) rose, as did two entry barrier measures, the capital to sales ratio (KO) and the advertising to sales ratio (ADVT), and the growth in industry output (GR). Geographic dispersion of markets, as measured by a higher value of GD, decreased price–cost margins. The remaining variables were non-significant: a measure of the proportion of central office employees (CEMP), the inventory–shipments ratio, the ratio of midpoint plant shipments to industry shipments (MID), and the ratio of fixed capital and inventory per dollar of shipments to midpoint plant shipments.

A problem with consensus studies is that they generally fail to take the other conditions (cited above) that affect the likelihood of coordination into account. For example, the size distribution of firms in an industry is generally approximated solely by the concentration ratio, despite the fact that high levels of measured concentration can coexist with a variety of possible size distributions. Different combinations may have very different implications for market power.

Barriers to entry have not been treated in a wholly satisfactory manner since the original Bain and Mann studies. Bain estimated barriers to entry as moderate to low, substantial, and very high on the basis of a detailed examination of each industry. Although his statistical treatment was not sophisticated, it was consistent with his theory, which suggested an interactive effect between barriers to entry and concentration. Weiss's subsequent regression analysis of the data explicitly embodied such interactions.

Later treatments have attempted to define measurable variables that can serve as proxies for various components of overall barriers to entry.[25] These have been of two types: some measure of optimal firm or plant size, or a measure of advertising intensity. Optimal firm or plant size in conjunction with industry size is held to be a proxy for economies of scale, while optimal firm or plant size with a measure of capital intensity is

[25] Weiss 1971; Intriligator et al. 1973; Scherer 1980, pp. 274–75.

held to be a proxy for capital requirement barriers. Advertising intensity is held to be a measure of product differentiation.

However, the optimal firm-size measures tend to be close to algebraically equivalent to the number of firms in an industry, and thus highly correlated with the industry concentration ratio. Optimal plant-size measures are also highly correlated with industry concentration ratios, thus raising some question about the appropriate use of these measures in regression analyses.[26] These variables and the advertising intensity variable have also been generally included in a simple linear model without the interaction effects, which are critical in Bain's theory and which the studies purport to test.

The period under study may also have a significant impact on the results, but is generally not explicitly considered. If the relation between industry profit rate and concentration exhibits systematic changes over the business cycle, then the portion of cycle or cycles chosen for study will affect the results. Weiss argues that large firms in concentrated industries are likely to raise prices less rapidly in inflationary periods than firms in more competitive industries. This tendency is strengthened in periods of price controls like 1971–1972 because large firms' pricing decisions are more closely monitored than those of other firms. Weiss suggests that for these reasons that such periods, including the period of this study, 1969–1973, are likely to be characterized by a weakening of the concentration–profitability relation.[27]

The expected impact of industry growth rates on the relationship of concentration to industry profit rates is ambiguous. Growth may be positively associated with profitability up to a point, while too rapid growth may reduce industry profit rates. In addition, the direction of causality in the short-term relationship between growth and firm profitability is ambiguous. The actions of firms such as increased sales effort, which are associated with firm profitability may also affect the industry

[26] Intriligator et al. 1973; Weiss 1974.
[27] Weiss 1974.

growth rates of sales. This occurs in addition to the expected direct effects of industry growth rates on firm profitability.

The use of industry profit rates rather than firm profit rates lumps together all firms in an industry regardless of size. There may be substantial differences in the statistical results obtained using industry and firm profit rates in regressions on concentration. In the case of a regression of industry profit rates on concentration a positive relation is expected. Highly concentrated industries are dominated by large firms with, on average, high rates of profit. Industries with low concentration tend to be populated by small firms and some large firms with lower mean rates of profit. As a result, average industry profitability which is weighted by firm size will be positively associated with concentration levels.

However, if the dependent variable is firm profitability instead of industry profitability, then the expected results are much less clear. A hypothesis consistent with the core–periphery hypothesis of chapter two is that large firm profitability will be high in concentrated industries and lower in less concentrated industries while small firm profitability is higher in less concentrated industries. If this is the case, then the overall regression results when the firm is the unit of measurement will depend on the relative profitability of successful small and large firms and of unsuccessful small and large firms. For example, if high-profit small firms tend to have profit rates less than high-profit large firms and there are not too many low-profit small firms in concentrated industries or too many relatively high-profit large firms in less concentrated industries, then there will be a positive relation between firm profitability and concentration. There are more conflicting forces at work in the relation of firm profitability to concentration than in the case of industry profitability.

The conceptual and statistical problem involves more than simply differences in the unit of measurement; it in fact turns upon the appropriateness of a particular unit to a hypothesis. Average industry profitability is the appropriate measure for a test of the strong collusion hypothesis that all firms' profit rates should be higher in an industry characterized by oligopolistic collusion. Just as clearly, the industry profit rate is not the appropriate measure for the hypothesis that the benefits of concentration accrue primarily to large firms; firm profit rates are required. The core–periphery hypothesis is of the latter type. It is about firm-specific characteristics and is most appropriately tested with firm profitability as the measure of performance.

The question of industry versus firm profit rates raises the more general problem of what simple linear relations between the industry profit rate and industry structure actually mean. The core–periphery hypothesis suggests that they do not mean a great deal, given the basic discontinuities in firm type between large and small firms in an industry.

A challenge to the consensus view within the field of industrial organization has been mounted by a series of critics who are concerned primarily with the related question of how firm size affects the relationship between concentration and profitability. They focus on the meaning of the positive statistical relationship between the level of industry concentration and an industry profit rate which is a weighted average of constituent firm profit rates. The challenge they raise is principally to the interpretation, within the traditional theoretical bounds of industrial organization, of that positive relationship as evidence that collusion exists. Their studies are reviewed in the two sections that follow.

SIZE, CONCENTRATION, AND PROFITABILITY

Most of the analyses of concentration and industry profit rates that explicitly incorporate firm size attempt to explain the concentration–profitability correlation by a "size effect." The source of the correlation is held to be simply that large firms own a larger fraction of the assets in highly concentrated industries. Since industry profit rates are weighted averages (by assets) of firm profit rates, in a concentrated industry the industry profit rate should be biassed toward large-firm profit rates. Insofar as large-firm profit rates are higher than small-firm profit rates, this bias will produce a positive overall concentration–profitability correlation across industries.[28]

Size-effect theorists have taken two general approaches. The first has been to analyze the profit–concentration relation in a regression context with an explicit attempt to remove the size effect. The assumption is that the correlation between concentration and profitability is a statistical artifact, which will disappear when analyzed with the appropriate techniques. The hypothesis is really a negative one: that there is no relation between concentration and industry profit rates.

Stanley Ornstein corrects for the bias introduced by the size effect of large firms by using a sample of just the largest firms in each industry.[29] As a result, the simple profitability–concentration correlation drops to what is in some years statistical insignificance. There are several sources of bias in this procedure, however. In industries with low seller concentration and a large number of small firms, taking only the profit rates of top firms as a measure of industry profit rates biasses upward the profit rate associated with the industry concentration level, as Ornstein also points out. In industries with high seller concentration and fewer small firms the profit rate is also biassed upwards by this procedure, but the bias must be less because large firms have a larger weight in the full universe of firms in such industries. In addition, the sample contains firms that existed for a thirteen-year period, which particularly in the case of low-concentration industries contains a bias toward the upper end of the profit distribution by eliminating firms that failed over the period. The overall result of the sampling procedure is to reduce the likelihood of finding a significant, positive concentration–profitability relationship in this sample when compared to the universe of all firms in the industries tested. Other than these sampling effects it is not clear what

---

[28] Asch and Marcus 1970, pp. 33–41; Demsetz 1973a, pp. 1–9; Demsetz 1973b; Ornstein 1972, pp. 519–41; Osborn 1970, pp. 15–26.

[29] Ornstein 1972.

has been demonstrated. In a test which uses firm rather than industry profit rates there is no reason to further adjust the sample to remove the size effect. Ornstein is testing only the narrow hypothesis that there is a positive relationship between concentration and the profitability of the leading firms in each industry. Most importantly, if the relationship of interest is that between profitability and concentration for all large firms then this is again not an appropriate test. The leading firms in the various industries are of widely varying sizes; these firms are not all large in an absolute sense. Thus Ornstein's results are not directly relevant to the size–concentration interaction of interest in the core–periphery analysis.

Peter Asch and Matihayu Marcus find preliminary support for the size-effect hypothesis when analyzing regression results of industry profit rates on concentration ratios, industry growth, and advertising intensity by size class.[30] The concentration coefficient is insignificant by size class but significant for the full sample. The general pattern of their results is in accord with the core–periphery hypothesis because there is a negative concentration coefficient for the smallest size class and a positive one for the largest size class although they are not statistically significant. The overall result is a positive and significant coefficient.

Asch and Marcus test the size-effect hypothesis by constructing a "size-expected" rate of return such that

$$\hat{r} = \Sigma_{j}\, \bar{r}_{j} a_{ij}$$

where $\bar{r}$ is the mean rate of return across industries for size class j and a_{ij} is the proportion of an industry i's assets held by firms in size class j. They regress this size-expected rate of return against concentration. The coefficient is positive but not significant. The effect of using an average size-class rate of return is to wash out precisely the relation that is of interest. It removes the concentration–size interaction. Since rate of return is held constant by asset class, industry rate of return is

[30] Asch and Marcus 1970.

simply a function of the proportions of each asset class represented in it. They isolate the size–rate of return relation. If there were a simple strictly monotonic size–rate of return relation across the economy and concentration were closely related to the proportion of industry assets held by large firms, we would expect their rate of return–concentration regression to be positive and significant. That the size–rate of return relation flattens out before the top size class probably contributes to their weak result. The results do provide indirect support for the hypothesis that it is the interaction between large size and concentration that explains large firms' superior performance in concentrated industries. If the only difference between industries with different levels of concentration were the proportions of different size classes of firms, then this test would isolate the true concentration–profitability relationship. However, since in the core–periphery hypothesis, large firms are expected to earn higher profits in highly concentrated industries than in less concentrated industries this test suppresses rather than isolates the relationship of central interest.

Richard Osborn corrects for the size effect in a somewhat different manner.[31] Instead of using the average profit rate by asset class across industries as did Asch and Marcus, he holds constant the proportion of each asset class across industries grouped by concentration level. "The average rates of return for firms of the same size were given the same weight in each concentration category. Weighting for the different sizes of firms was made the same for all categories and was based on the actual percentages of total assets owned by the combined firms of each size." In effect Osborn seems to use the actual average profit rate by size class within each industry but attaches a constant cross-industry weight to each size-class profit rate to construct industry average profit rates. After his adjustment Osborn's results show, by broad concentration categories, that the positive concentration–rate of return relation for his unweighted sample is reversed. This test is also not relevant to

[31] Osborn 1970.

understanding the concentration–size–rate of return interaction because it assumes away one aspect of the interaction. Osborn's test attempts to isolate the concentration–rate of return relation. Since large firms control a larger share of assets in concentrated industries this procedure merely flattens out the concentration–rate of return function. The weights described increase the weight given to the higher profit rates of large firms in low-concentration industries compared to their actual weight and conversely decrease the weight of large firms in high-concentration industries compared to their actual weights. They also increase the weight of low and negative small-firm profit rates in high-concentration industries as well as increasing the weight of higher small-firm profit rates in low-concentration industries, again compared to their actual weights.

If there were a positive relationship between concentration and rate of return for large firms and a positive relation for most other size groups, then this test should show positive results. However, if there were a flat or negative relation for the other size groups then this test would not show positive results. Thus Osborn's negative results do not provide grounds to reject the core–periphery hypothesis that there is a positive concentration–profitability relationship for large firms but not for smaller firms.

This first approach to the size effect treats the relationship between size, concentration, and profitability as a purely statistical problem. It makes more sense to understand it as representing a real phenomenon: the effect of the interaction between size and concentration on profitability. All of the results are consistent with or are not adequate to reject the hypothesis that there is a positive rate of return–concentration relation for large firms and a nonsignificant or negative relation for small firms. None of these studies explicitly focusses on the concentration–rate of return relation by size class; they reweight by various factors, but focus on the overall concentration–rate of return relation. The reason for the overall positive concentration–industry rate of return correlation usually reported is that large firms dominate concentrated industries and that the performance of large firms in concentrated industries is better than the performance of large firms in less-concentrated industries and of small firms in unconcentrated as well as concentrated industries. The studies above do serve to make the point that concentration by itself does not really mean very much. It is impossible, in fact, to separate concentration from large firms. There is in effect no such thing as a highly concentrated industry (at the three-digit IRS level used in this study) dominated by small firms. As a result it does not make sense to try to separate size and concentration statistically.

The second approach of the size-effect theorists, whose best-known advocate is Harold Demsetz, is more substantive. Demsetz uses empirical results on the interaction between firm size, concentration levels, and firm and industry profit rates to counter a traditional part of the theory explaining the relation between concentration and profitability. That theory provides, in the "strong collusion" position as constructed by Demsetz, that collusion can proceed successfully only with all firms in an industry involved. If this type of collusion is the mechanism required to translate concentration into higher profits, then all firms in a concentrated industry should have equal and above-average profit rates regardless of size. Demsetz argues that this should be the case unless there are differences in cost between firms under the collusive agreement, or differences in price. For example, some firms receive a higher price for a differentiated and presumably superior product.[32]

The strong collusion argument has several clear, testable implications in Demsetz's view. The first is that all firms in an industry should have equal rates of profit unless some firms have an efficiency advantage. The second is that both large and small firms' profit rates should vary positively with the level of concentration.

Demsetz demonstrates that the relationship between concentration and profitability is not constant across size classes

[32] Demsetz 1973a.

for 1963 and 1969. It is positive for the largest firms and negative or insignificant for smaller firms. Additional regressions indicate that the difference in profit rates between the largest firms and three subsets of smaller firms is a positive function of the level of concentration. Demsetz takes this as evidence that not only is the strong collusion hypothesis not supported but that the efficiency hypothesis is supported; large firms became large as a result of efficiency and earn higher profits as a result of that efficiency. Demsetz does not explain what it is about concentrated industries that makes large firms more efficient there and thus does not provide a convincing explanation of his results.[33]

The results reported by Demsetz are consistent with the hypothesis of this study: large firms gain from their dominant position in concentrated industries while small firms are more likely to do well in unconcentrated industries in competition primarily with other firms of similar size. The core–periphery hypothesis is that there are significant heterogeneities in the population of firms that contribute to market power for large firms within concentrated industries and at the same time prevent small firms from sharing in the benefits of that market power.

Marshall Hall and Leonard Weiss analyze the relationship between concentration, profitability, and size in a somewhat different manner. They focus on the size–profitability relation and include concentration in a regression model to test for the independent effects of market power. The firm rate of return is regressed on industry concentration levels, firm size, and several other variables. Hall and Weiss argue that their results support the hypothesis that while concentration does have such an independent effect on profitability, its contribution is minor compared with size.[34]

In part, the magnitude of the concentration coefficient in their regression estimates is a result of a bias imparted by their

---

[33] Ibid.; see also "Summary" section of this chapter for further discussion.
[34] Hall and Weiss 1967, pp. 318–31.

sample selection. The bias is similar to that noted in the analysis of Ornstein's study, in that Hall and Weiss use only the largest or "optimal"–sized firms in each industry. Further, given the interaction between size and concentration, it is not clear that it is possible to test for the "independent" effects of each. In fact, firm size and concentration levels are collinear in their sample. Both factors suggest the significance the authors impute to their results that size is the principal determinant of profitability in the size–concentration nexus, is too great.

William Shepherd also tests for the independent effects of size, using a regression model that incorporates the full range of market structure elements including size, market share, and concentration. The coefficient of firm size is negative although not consistently significant. The study suffers from one of the defects of the Hall and Weiss study, in that market share, concentration, and size are collinear and the study also includes other variables that are probably collinear with the size measure.[35]

The principal conclusion which can be drawn from these studies is that there is a significant size–concentration–profitability interaction which throws the interpretation of the simple concentration–profitability analyses into doubt. This interaction appears as the empirically significantly different relation between concentration and profitability for large firms and for small firms. A second conclusion to be drawn from these methodologically variegated studies is that this interaction has no generally agreed upon or well-demonstrated meaning within the framework of industrial organization analysis. The argument advanced implicitly or explicitly by the various size-effect theorists is that size is an individual firm characteristic and that any positive relation between profitability and size can therefore be attributed to firms' individual efficiency rather than to market power based on a group characteristic like concentration. This issue will be taken up in

[35] Shepherd 1972, pp. 35–37; for further analysis of this article see the "Market Share and Profitability" section below.

more detail in the "Summary" section below, where it is argued that the interpretations of both the consensus literature and size-effect literature share a basic perspective and that the theory of core and periphery provides an alternative explanation for the same results.

MARKET SHARE AND PROFITABILITY

A second, less well-developed literature has also questioned the consensus view on concentration and profitability. These studies examine the relationship between market share, or relative size, and profitability in the context of the interdependent effects of size and concentration on profitability. The empirical results of this literature are again fairly consistent. There is a positive significant simple relation between market share and firm profit rate. There is less agreement on how this simple positive relation is affected by firm size or industry concentration and what the significance of the overall pattern of interactions is.

Bradley Gale's study shows a positive significant relation between market share and profit rate. Gale shows further in an interaction analysis that the effect of relative size, measured by market share, on firm profitability is substantially enhanced by high levels of concentration. While market share in isolation has a positive effect on profitability, its effect is much stronger in concentrated industries than in unconcentrated industries.[36] In effect this represents a test of the difference between core and noncore large firms because Gale's sample was drawn from the top several hundred firms in the manufacturing sector. It suggests that large firms benefit more from their relative size in concentrated industries, where oligopolistic conduct within a dominant group can take place, than in less-concentrated industries where such conduct is less likely.

Gale shows a similar effect of absolute size on the relationship between market share and profitability. The positive ef-

[36] Gale 1972, pp. 412–23.

fect of market share on profitability was also substantially enhanced by large firm size. The relationship is significantly stronger for larger firms than for smaller firms. This represents a test of the effect of differences in absolute size, among the largest firms in the economy, on the advantage bestowed by large relative size, or market share. The results do not bear directly on the differences between core and periphery but suggest again that absolute size interacts in a significant way with relative size.

In a later article Ben Branch and Gale use a different, business-unit-level data base to explore similar relationships. They show a positive significant bivariate relation between market share and business-unit profitability and a positive simple bivariate relation between concentration and profitability. A multiple regression of profitability on both market share and concentration results in a positive significant coefficient on market share and a negative non-significant coefficient on concentration. The authors conclude from this result that "It is market share not concentration which influences profitability."[37]

In Branch and Gale's analysis, a share–concentration interaction term was not significant when added in either the simple bivariate share regression or the multiple regression. This is inconsistent both with Gale's earlier results and with the expectation of this study. The explanation may lie in the fact that the interaction term in Branch and Gale (1979) is multiplicative while the term in Gale (1972) is a dummy for high and low concentration. The hypothesis of a discrete change in slope is more consistent with the hypothesis of this study than a continuous relation. Finally, the Branch and Gale study tests a market share–firm size interaction. The interaction term in this case was a slope dummy and the coefficient was positive in accord with expectation and Gale's earlier results.

John Kwoka analyzes the relative explanatory power of

[37] Branch and Gale 1979.

concentration and market share on industry profitability.[38] Kwoka disaggregates four-firm concentration ratios into individual market shares and compares the explanatory power of incremental shares on industry profitability. His results indicate that the combined shares of the two leading firms are better explanators than any other combination of shares. In fact the sign associated with the third share was negative although insignificant and the fourth and subsequent shares are also insignificant. The meaning of his results for the third and fourth share are not fully clear. However, his results support the hypothesis of a positive effect of both concentration and market share on industry profitability without distinguishing between them.

Shepherd tests several hypotheses related to the interacting effects of profitability, market share, concentration, and firm size.[39] In a regression of firm profit rate on market share the coefficient of market share is positive and significant. In a similar simple regression on concentration the slope coefficient is also positive and significant but smaller than the share coefficient. Both of these results are in accord with the expectations outlined above. Since market share and concentration are highly collinear in Shepherd's sample, they are not used in the same equation. Finally, when size is included in multiple regressions of firm profitability on market share and related variables—advertising intensity, growth, and others—its coefficient is uniformly negative and sometimes significant. This is not really contrary to expectation although it contrasts with the findings of Hall and Weiss. Shepherd's sample consists of 231 of the top 500 manufacturing firms by total profits between 1960 and 1969. The expectation about the relation of profitability to size in a sample of the largest firms in the economy is that it would be anywhere from mildly positive to mildly negative depending on the period and other factors (see "Size and Profitability" section).

[38] Kwoka 1979, pp. 101–109.
[39] Shepherd 1972.

Although not explicitly acknowledged in this literature, market share and industry concentration are two related measures of the same phenomenon, relative firm size. Market share captures one dimension of relative firm size within an industry, the firm share of sales. Four-firm concentration ratios measure the size in sales of the top four firms relative to the industry; such concentration ratios are by definition just the simple sum of the individual market shares of the top firms in an industry.

In a sample with a relatively broad range of market shares, as is the case with the sample of Branch and Gale's study, a weak positive relation between concentration and profitability is expected for the following reasons. High-share firms will tend to be in relatively concentrated industries almost by definition. Low-share firms can be in both high and low concentration industries although logic would suggest that those in low-concentration industries should outnumber those in high-concentration industries. In the sample of Branch and Gale, in fact there is a simple correlation coefficient of 0.27 between share and concentration. While this is a lower correlation than some other samples, the evidence is at least consistent with the hypothesis that market share and concentration measure closely related phenomena and that dramatic conclusions such as Branch and Gale's are not warranted.

The efficiency argument advanced by Branch and Gale is almost identical to that made by Demsetz, although couched in terms of market share rather than asset size. The logic of both positions is the following: If the unit of analysis can be reduced from the industry level to the level of the firm (or to subsets of firms arranged by a critical firm-level variable in the case of the size-effect theorists) then any association between the rate of profit and variables representing individual firm characteristics can be attributed to efficiency rather than to a group dynamic like collusion. The critical assumption is that market power is uniquely a function of a group dynamic that depends principally on the level of industry concentration and that individual firm performance, which is not statistically related to concentration, is uniquely a function of efficiency characteristics.

The core–periphery analysis suggests that market power depends on both individual firm characteristics and on a group dynamic. They are equally important and, moreover, cannot be separated in a typical oligopoly situation because their interaction is also an important ingredient in market power. Gale's results on the concentration–market share interaction effect on profitability are consistent with this interpretation.

SUMMARY

A debate has emerged within the industrial organization literature about the meaning of the empirical results on concentration, market share, size, and profitability reviewed above.[40] The limits of the debate, which can be broadly construed as taking place between liberals and conservatives, are defined by traditional views of industrial structure and competition. Both sides share a common analytical framework but disagree over the question of how much weight to give to efficiency and market power in interpreting the effect of individual firm attributes on both firm and industry rates of profit. The core–periphery hypothesis offers a different view of industrial structure and competition from that which defines the liberal–conservative debate. The empirical results offered by both sides are consistent with the core–periphery view.

The liberal position on the relationship between market share, concentration, and profitability is that share and concentration represent two separable forces which affect the profit rate. Concentration serves as a reasonable proxy for oligopolistic collusion while share may represent efficiency.[41] In this view, the large number of empirical studies of the concentration–profitability relation indicate that there is a robust relationship between concentration and industry profit rates and

---

[40] See, for example, Goldschmid et al. 1974.
[41] Weiss 1974; Scherer 1980, pp. 267–95.

that the collusion/monopoly power hypothesis is upheld. The liberals admit, however, that there is some doubt about exactly what the concentration–industry profitability results mean when market share and absolute firm size are introduced.

The conservatives first raised and embraced the views that gave rise to this doubt. They argue that both concentration and higher industry profit rates are the result primarily of various efficiencies in operation by large firms.[42] In their view large firms gain a large market share as a result of economies of scale and/or because they sell a "superior" product. The association between concentration and industry profit rates is a result of large firm efficiency and the size effect rather than any monopoly power or collusion. The conservatives argue that market share is a proxy for efficiency because share is associated with individual firms, in contrast to concentration. A positive association between firm profit rates and market share, in this view, supports the efficiency interpretation over the collusion interpretation.

The liberals respond to these two lines of attack by arguing first that there is good reason to expect the benefits of collusion to accrue primarily to the leading firms in an industry. Large firms choose prices to maximize their own rate of return and can ignore the lower prices of small firms because they have no significant impact on the market. In addition many small firms are suboptimal, high-cost producers attracted to the industry by high profit rates that can earn only a "normal" rate of return upon entry even with higher prices.[43]

The liberal response to the market share argument is to accede to the probable association between market share and efficiency but to argue that there is an independent concentration–profitability relation that persists despite the effect of market share on profitability. The liberals also point out that dominant high-share firms may gain some of their higher returns from control over price as a result of advertising created

[42] Demsetz 1973b; Brozen 1971.
[43] Weiss 1974; Scherer 1980, pp. 281–86.

product differentiation which suggests a barrier to entry rather than lower costs or a superior product.[44] In this view the coefficients of market share and concentration in a multiple regression, with profit rate as the dependent variable, provide the appropriate test of the relative strengths of efficiency and collusion as they affect profitability, although they do not specify whether it is the firm or industry profit rate.[45]

Central to both liberal and conservative positions is the argument that collusion in a broad sense is the mechanism by which industry profit rates are increased in the presence of concentration. Further, both argue that the effects of concentration and market share or firm size on industry and firm profitability are separable. In fact, these points of view are remarkably similar in their basic assumptions. Their difference lies in the relatively narrow area of how to interpret specific empirical results witin the agreed-upon framework.

Liberals and conservatives share the critical assumption that the concept of a homogeneous product industry is the appropriate theoretical approach to the problems of disentangling the effects of collusion and efficiency.[46] The concept has two important elements which are relevant here, that all firms in an industry produce the same product and that all firms in an industry produce subject to the same cost function. If all firms produce identical products, then most firms, depending on the industry's cost structure, will benefit from the higher prices introduced via collusion. The ability to make a clear distinction between the effects of market share and concentration on firm profitability also depends on this assumption. If all firms produce identical output, variations in profitability with market share can more readily be associated with economies of scale than is the case if they do not.

In the homogeneous product industry model, interfirm differences in profitability derive from interfirm variation in the

---

[44] Ibid.

[45] Weiss 1974, pp. 226–27.

[46] See, for example, the discussion in Scherer 1980, pp. 282–85.

differences between costs and price. As a result, large firms' profitability advantage must derive from lower costs and/or higher prices. For both camps part of the advantage lies in lower costs, generally associated with efficiency. Smoothly declining industry costs curves of various shapes can be drawn to illustrate this large-firm advantage. The implication is that causality runs for technical reasons from increased output (per plant) to decreased costs and thus to higher profitability for the large firms that own the plants.

The liberals' explanation of size-related profit differences within industries characterized by collusion is presented in terms of the homogeneous product model. They argue that the largest firms in the industry are of "optimal size" and that the lower profits earned by smaller firms are a result of inefficiency necessarily associated with their small size. If a simple cost curve can approximate the cost structure of the industry then it can explain the lower profits of small firms, which produce in the high cost end of the curve.[47]

Given the homogeneous product industry model and empirical results about large firms, this technical explanation for large firms' advantages and for the existence of concentration follows logically. The argument adopts with few caveats the conservative interpretation that industries characterized both by high concentration ratios and by high levels of profitability for the largest firms have cost curves which decline continuously, while more competitive industries have cost curves that are flat above some minimum output.

The liberal argument about optimal size is thus quite similar to the conservative size-effect argument; only large firms benefit from concentration. However, while the conservatives take this as evidence that collusion is not the explanation, the liberals do not. The liberals argue that while oligopolists' position and profitability depend in part on lower costs, their position also makes possible higher prices, which further increase their profitability and which have nothing directly to do with

[47] Ibid., pp. 280–85.

lower costs. These higher prices are a result of collusion in various forms and/or of barriers to entry.[48]

The explanation for the continued advantages of the more "efficient" firms within the liberal view of collusion theory is that the collusive agreement, when successful, prohibits significant share changes as the price for stability and high prices for all. Collusion as it is typically used in oligopoly theory and in industrial organization theory implies an agreement, of various possible degrees of formality, to restrict competition, which requires constant policing by member firms in order to ensure compliance.[49] Collusion depends on conscious enforcement of an agreement in order to maintain share, and thus price and profit stability. The cost of information about prices and market shares required for effective policing declines with the number of firms party to the agreement. Thus collusion is more effective in concentrated markets and profits should also be higher there, subject to various caveats.

Small firms may be excluded from the benefits of higher prices either because the elevated price is just adequate for a normal profit over and above their high costs or because barriers to entry protect only the dominant firms. In the absence of barriers there is no reason why small firms cannot simply expand output, reduce costs, and compete actively with larger firms.

In order to compete with efficiency as an explanation for firm-specific profit rate advantages such barriers to entry must be associated uniquely with individual firms. The barrier with this characteristic generally cited in liberal discussions of the issue is product differentiation via advertising expenditures. Advertising and the resultant product differentiation in consumer goods industries are associated with single firms, can provide a barrier to the expansion of small firms in the industry and to new entry, and can allow differentiating firms to raise prices and earn higher profits.

[48] Ibid.; Weiss 1974.
[49] See, for example, Stigler 1964.

The possibility of product differentiation violates the assumption of homogeneous product industries but it does so in a limited way. The possibility of differentiation is generally adduced to demonstrate that higher prices as well as lower costs may be associated with individual dominant firms. In a sense the potential for higher prices is simply added on to the homogeneous industry construct without affecting other elements of commonality between firms, most importantly the identical cost curves upon which the efficiency argument rests.

The homogeneous product industry model provides the analytical basis for attempts to construe market power as purely a collective phenomenon in the form of collusion while associating individual firm attributes, like size and market power, with efficiency. However the mere association of an individual firm's attributes with enhanced profitability does not establish efficiency as the underlying cause of concentration or of higher profits in the absence of the homogeneous industry assumptions.

From the core–periphery perspective the homogeneous product industry is a misleading abstraction when applied to the set of theoretical and empirical problems addressed in the literature of concentration, size, market share, and rate of return. It is the hypothesis of this study that there are basic differences between core and periphery firms which make analytical reliance on a homogeneous product model more misleading than would be the case if only the universe of very large firms were to be considered. It is hypothesized that core firms have broader product lines, are more diversified and more vertically integrated than periphery firms. These basic structural differences are augmented by differences in competitive strategies between core and periphery firms. It is hypothesized that, both more intensively and extensively, core firms advertise, create new products, engage in research and development which produce new products and production processes, diversify via investment and acquisition, and establish extensive distribution and marketing systems. Core firms have the ability to make and to benefit from investments not available to periphery firms. Periphery firms either do not or cannot pursue these strategies or do so less systematically and on a much smaller scale than do core firms. In the core–periphery view, core firms are not simply larger undifferentiated masses of capital which operate further out along a smoothly sloping industry cost function, they are qualitatively different from periphery firms.

Analyses utilizing the homogeneous product industry model implicitly lump the core firm advantages deriving from size and market share under the rubric of economies of scale, which they confuse with efficiency, and conclude that there is a technical basis for high levels of profitability. Exactly why it is that efficiency leads to higher profits when large size is conjoined with high levels of concentration than when large size exists independently is not well explained by the conservatives. The liberals argue that while efficiency results in large size and higher profit rates, that any additional profits which accrue to large firms in concentrated industries over large firms in unconcentrated industries represent the sole contribution of market power.

In order to argue that the advantages of large firms are primarily a result of superior efficiency, it is necessary to interpret the evident advantages of size as representing real efficiencies as opposed to pecuniary economies. The empirical evidence, based on a wide variety of techniques, suggests that production economies are of little significance in explaining current levels of industrial concentration. A variety of other factors including most simply the reduced competition associated with substantial joint market share, large firm advantages unrelated to production efficiency in advertising, access to capital, input procurement, and distribution, plus the complex interaction between levels of concentration and strategic competitive decisions about plant additions and pricing, for example, provide the basis for the superior performance of large firms with market power.[50]

[50] For a review of the evidence on economies of scale see Scherer 1974, pp. 16–54.

None of the range of large-firm advantages, with the possible exception of these production economies, can be unequivocally associated with efficiency. While there may be unit cost savings associated with certain large investments over smaller scale investments, the question is whether they are real resource savings and whether they are necessarily associated with large firms. What is it, for example, that prevents small firms from investing in plants of optimal scale? For example, it is probably not necessary from a pure efficiency standpoint to have large national distribution/marketing networks owned by large firms. They could be owned by independent firms and serve the same function. A large part of the reason that large firms created them and continue to own them derives from considerations of market power. An independent distribution company would have substantial power vis-à-vis a producer, and other large firms which did make such an investment would also gain a significant advantage.

In the core–periphery view, the dominance of an industry by core firms depends on individual firm market power derived from absolute as well as relative size, which together make possible the collective phenomenon of corespective behavior. Concentration or joint market share cannot be separated either analytically or statistically in a meaningful sense from the large absolute and relative size of the firms that together hold a concentrated share of industry sales. In the core–periphery view, market power results from large absolute size together with substantial joint market share and is not purely a collective phenomenon. The collective and individual components of market power are interdependent. Large absolute or relative firm size without concentration is not enough to create core firms because no firm or group of firms has a large enough share of the market to permit corespective behavior. Concentration or large joint market share is also not adequate without large absolute size because a market dominated by small firms could be entered by large firms if the profit rate was an adequate lure.

Absolute size of individual firms constitutes a critical barrier to entry to the core group for other firms both within and outside particular industries. Individual firm profit-maximizing behavior results in barriers to entry to the core group while core firm pricing behavior which is more directly a function of the group dynamic also contributes to entry barriers and the perpetuation of core firms' position in an industry. Core firms' market share and market power depend on their pursuit of a competitive strategy consistent with corespective behavior, which is in turn dependent on the retaliatory power of individual core firms. Market share, size, and the group dynamic cannot be neatly separated.

There is no good empirical evidence to support the claim that large firms are uniformly more efficient than smaller firms or that efficiency is positively correlated with firm size at all, above some minimum size. In the absence of that evidence and without the assumptions of the homogeneous product model there is no basis for the assumption that size and/or market share are neatly separable from market power. As a result there is a strong presumption that core firm profitability results to a significant extent from pecuniary economies rather than real economies of scale. Higher profits represent in large part returns to the combination of size and joint market share which form the basis for market power.

RISK

Firm-specific risk has been approached conceptually in two ways in the empirical industrial organization literature, as business risk and as financial risk.[51] Business risk is the risk, to a firm, associated with variations in a firm's rate of return on assets. Financial risk is the risk, to stockholders, associated with variations in the return on equity. Firms with relatively severe fluctuations in income face the ultimate risk of failure as well as the threat to investment plans and competitive viability associated with an unstable supply of funds. Fluctuations in return on equity, which can, of course, derive from fluctuations

[51] Brigham 1977, pp. 555–61.

in overall income, increase the risk to stockholders that they will not earn their expected rate of return and may result in an increased cost of external capital. Business risk, because it is associated with changes in the rate of return to the firm as a whole, is of primary interest in this study. However, financial risk, insofar as it derives from or is related to business risk, is also of interest.

Business risk is a function of both industry conditions and market power. It is hypothesized here that core firms can use their market power to offset some industry-specific risks and can withstand effects of such risks more successfully than periphery firms; the market power of core firms allows them to improve the terms of the expected tradeoff between risk and rate of return and to earn both higher and less risky profits than other firms. The simple relation between profit rates and their riskiness is shaped by structural forces, primarily the interacting effects of absolute firm size and dominance of particular markets. The result is that there is no single underlying tradeoff for all firms, with a single functional form, between risk of any kind and rate of return. The bifurcated process of profit rate formation carries over to the determination of the full risk-adjusted rate of return.

This section reviews the relevant parts of the empirical industrial organization literature and attempts to demonstrate that these empirical results are consistent with the hypotheses of core and periphery. The review will focus on three widely used measures of risk: temporal variability of firm profit rates, leverage, and the cross-sectional variability of firm profit rates.

Although the empirical tests in the literature uniformly assume a homogeneous tradeoff across firms, variations in sample selection and correlations tested provide results that are consistent with the hypothesis that there are different relations for core and periphery firms. For example, in interindustry tests of a firm-specific tradeoff between rate of return and a risk measure, a size effect analogous to that discussed earlier may appear. If there is a strong negative relation between rate of return and leverage for periphery firms and a weaker negative relation for core firms, and if periphery firms have both lower profit rates on average and lower leverage, then the relation between rate of return and leverage measured across all firms may be positive.

Temporal Profit Rate Variability

Empirical studies of temporal business risk have examined the relation between risk and several other variables of interest to this analysis: size, concentration, and profitability.

The evidence on firm size and temporal risk over a variety of samples points consistently to a negative relation.[52] Only H. O. Stekler finds a different pattern, an "inverse U-shape," which can, however, be attributed to the fact that only profitable firms were included in his test.[53] Explanations in the literature for this negative relation include the greater diversification of large firms, sticky prices of large firms and the greater ability of large firms to withstand fluctuations in the level of economic activity.

Insofar as core firms in a statistical sense dominate the performance of large firms as a group, this result is consistent with the interpretation that core firms have lower temporal variation in their profits. There is no evidence that bears on the claim that the relation between profit rate and temporal risk is significantly different between large and small firms, however, because firm data is either grouped into size classes or covers only the largest firms.

The limited evidence on the relation of temporal risk to the concentration of the firm's home industry poses more problems for analysis. In general, bivariate regressions of temporal risk on concentration show negative slope coefficients.[54] Simple tabular analyses indicate the same negative association.[55]

[52] Samuels and Smyth 1968, pp. 127–39; Sherman 1968, pp. 156–72; Stekler 1963, pp. 88–100; Stekler 1964, pp. 1183–93; Winn 1977, pp. 157–63.
[53] Stekler 1964.
[54] Shepherd 1972; Winn 1975, pp. 82–86.
[55] Sherman 1968, pp. 166–72; Winn 1977.

However, when Daryl Winn includes firm size and capital–output ratios as independent variables, the sign of the concentration coefficient becomes positive and significant while the coefficients on size and capital–output ratio are negative.[56]

Interpretation of this change in sign relies on the relation between size and concentration discussed above. Size and concentration are collinear, especially in a sample like Winn's composed of 736 of the largest manufacturing corporations. Concentration is also collinear with the capital–output ratio. It is not clear how to interpret the positive sign of the concentration variable, given this collinearity and the bivariate regression results, and the significance of the individual coefficients on concentration and size in such a linear regression is also not clear.[57] It is the combination of firm size and industry concentration that is expected to have a powerful effect on both profitability and the variability of profits.

The negative bivariate association between concentration and temporal variability is consistent with the hypothesis that core firms dominate concentrated industries and successfully use their market power to reduce profit rate fluctuations. Richard Caves and B. S. Yamey hypothesize a positive relation between concentration and temporal profit rate variability due to the expected periodic breakdown of collusive agreements in concentrated industries, which should raise both the level and variability of large firm profit rates.[58] However, in the core–periphery view core firm patterns of corespective behavior are not expected to break down with sufficient regularity to produce a significant increase in those fluctuations.

The also limited evidence on temporal risk and firm profitability appears to be equally contradictory; two studies show a positive relation while a third shows a negative association. The I. N. Fisher and G. R. Hall, and Paul Cootner and Daniel

---

[56] Winn 1975, p. 85; Winn 1977.

[57] Winn 1975, p. 85, comments on his own results: "Obviously, the results are heavily influenced by positive collinearity of concentration with firm size and capital intensity."

[58] Caves and Yamey 1971, pp. 513–17.

Holland studies have several elements in common that contribute to a plausible explanation for their finding of a positive relation.[59] This explanation lies in the probable combined effects of sample selection and period chosen. Both studies use samples which include firms in the upper-middle to large-size classes for a fifteen-year period, 1946 to 1960 in one case and 1950 to 1964 in the other. The selection of firms which were in continuous existence over these full fifteen-year periods may impart a bias similar to that created by excluding all nonprofitable firms. Rates of failure are strongly and inversely related to firm size, so when nonprofitable firms are excluded the relation between size and profitability becomes negative. A similar result obtains if all failed firms are excluded from the sample.[60] When this negative relation between size and profitability is combined with the well-established negative relation between size and the temporal variability of profits, a positive relation between profitability and temporal profit variability is expected, *ceteris paribus*. Thus, the meaning and significance of that positive result in these two studies are thrown into some doubt.

The third study, by Winn, is also for a relatively long time period, 1960 to 1968, but because the period was one of relatively sustained expansion the bias introduced by using only surviving firms is probably reduced.[61] This inference is borne out by a closer examination of Winn's results, which show both a positive relation between size and profitability and a negative relation between size and the temporal variability of profits. As a result, the relation between profitability and its temporal variance is expected to be negative, *ceteris paribus*, and Winn's results show a negative relation. The reduced sample bias reflected in the positive size–profitability association is

[59] Cootner and Holland 1970, pp. 211–26; Fisher and Hall 1969, pp. 79–92.

[60] This is the result obtained on a similar sample by Samuels and Smyth 1968.

[61] Winn 1975, p. 80.

consistent with Winn's results being closer to the "true" relation than the previous two studies.

Another way of understanding the divergent results is as a reflection of a size effect. The samples of both the Cootner and Holland and Fisher and Hall studies represent what can be interpreted as a more homogeneous core firm population than Winn's sample. The former samples are drawn from a narrower group of the largest corporations and they are the members of this group which survived over a fifteen-year period. Winn's sample is drawn from a significantly larger cross-section of large firms, has a reduced bias toward successful firms, and as a result probably incorporates a broader spectrum of both size and market power.

If there are two distinct functional relationships between rate of return and temporal risk for core and periphery firms then the positive relation of the first two studies is consistent with a positive intracore tradeoff. The negative relation of Winn's study is consistent with a relation estimated across both core and periphery in which the subrelationships can be characterized as a less positive relationship among more profitable core firms and a more positive relationship among less profitable periphery firms.

The evidence overall on temporal profit rate variability and various market structure measures, while not powerful, is consistent with the theory of core and periphery. The negative relation between size and temporal profit variability, and the probable negative relations between concentration and temporal profit variability and profit rate and temporal profit variability are consistent with the hypothesis that large firms in concentrated industries face a more favorable rate of return–risk tradeoff than other firms and earn both higher and less variable profit rates.

Leverage

Leverage, defined (consistent with the empirical literature) as the ratio of equity to assets, is a frequently used measure of the risk associated with individual firms. There are two dominant hypotheses about the expected relation of leverage to firm profitability. The first, or financial risk hypothesis, is that leverage, equity divided by assets, is an inverse measure of the riskiness of a firm's capital structure and should therefore be negatively related to the rate of return on equity.[62]

It is a basic precept of corporate finance that as the proportion of debt in a firm's capital structure increases, *ceteris paribus* the risk to the firm increases because the amount of fixed obligations as a proportion of income increases. If a debt payment is missed bankruptcy can follow. The risk to equity-holders rises with the proportion of debt because holders of fixed income securities are paid before holders of equity in the event of liquidation, and because the likely fluctuations in return on equity increase with the proportion of debt since any given change in firm income will produce wider swings in return on equity as equity shrinks as a proportion of total assets.[63] Thus, the first hypothesis is that holders of equity in a firm with a large proportion of debt bear more risk than equity-holders in firms with a smaller proportion of debt and that they are compensated for this risk by higher returns, on average. The first hypothesis also implies, although less strongly, that firms bear more risk as the proportion of debt rises and that all the owners of capital are compensated for this risk. The implication is a negative relation between return on equity and the ratio of equity to assets and between return on total assets and leverage.

The second, or business risk, hypothesis is that firms choose a capital structure to offset their business risk, which is one of the factors held constant in the first hypothesis.[64] Business risk derives from uncertainty about the stream of income to the firm, which derives in turn from the business environment of the firm. Firms with higher than average business risk will

---

[62] Brigham 1977, pp. 555–61; Hall and Weiss 1967.

[63] Brigham 1977, pp. 555–89.

[64] Ibid., p. 556; Gale 1972.

choose a capital structure with a higher than average ratio of equity to assets and vice versa. The predicted correlation between the ratio of equity to assets and the rate of return is positive, exactly the opposite of that predicted by the first hypothesis. In sum, the second hypothesis is that the ratio of equity to assets is positively associated with business risk and because the owners of capital must be compensated for increased risk-bearing, there will be a positive association between leverage and the rate of return, measured on either equity or total assets.

From the perspective of core and periphery, the second, or business-risk hypothesis appears more plausible. Given the hypothesized significant differences in market power and therefore business risk between core and periphery firms, a theory which explicitly accounts for the way in which such differences affect the choice of financial structure is required. In addition the business-risk hypothesis clearly does not contradict the financial-risk hypothesis. Rather, the business-risk hypothesis subsumes the financial-risk hypothesis by assuming that externally imposed business risk determines a firm's choice of financial risk and therefore the nature of the relation between leverage and rate of return. By contrast the financial-risk hypothesis assumes that the choice of a financial risk position is made without regard to external risk conditions, and is therefore itself the critical determinant of the shape of the relationship between leverage and rate of return.

The empirical evidence is ambiguous. Several studies have found that in a regression of return on equity on the equity–assets ratio and other variables, across a sample of the largest firms, that the slope coefficient is positive and significant in accord with the second hypothesis.[65] However, an anomalous finding by Hall and Weiss spurred a new line of reasoning. They found that although the coefficient of leverage was posi-

---

[65] Gale 1972; Hall and Weiss 1967. Both Hurdle 1974 and Baker 1973 obtain similar results using OLS and opposite results using 2SLS although neither offers a convincing explanation for this reversal.

tive in a regression with concentration as a continuous variable, when concentration was introduced as a dummy variable,
the sign of the coefficient on leverage was negative in each concentration category.

Hall and Weiss, and Caves in a later article, take this as evidence for the first hypothesis.[66] They argue that although market power, represented by concentration, has allowed dominant firms to reverse the risk–return tradeoff when compared
to other firms, that the negative relation (consistent with the
first hypothesis) between the rate of return and leverage still
holds within market power categories and that it holds implicitly across all firms within an industry or for all firms with
comparable business risk. In addition, Caves, and Hall and
Weiss take the coexistence, on average, of high return on equity and high equity–asset ratios for firms in concentrated industries as evidence that these firms take part of the advantages of their market position in the form of a less risky capital
structure rather than in even higher profits.[67] It follows, according to their hypothesis, that in the absence of such risk reduction, the first risk hypothesis would hold across all firms.

If the concentration dummy variable is interpreted to have
controlled for interindustry differences in business risk, then
the regression merely isolated the negative intrabusiness-risk
class or intraindustry relation between leverage and rate of return consistent with the first hypothesis. This interpretation is
made more plausible by the fact that because the sample includes only dominant firms or "firms of optimal scale," in each
industry, it would seem difficult to separate the independent
effects of market power and industry membership on business
risk. That is, sample selection makes the assumed congruence
of industry concentration group and business-risk class reasonable.

If the "anomalous" Hall and Weiss results have isolated the

[66] Caves 1970; Hall and Weiss 1967.
[67] Sullivan 1974 also argues for this hypothesis; Melicher et al. 1976 find no
significant relationship between levels of concentration and leverage.

intrabusiness-risk class risk-rate of return relationship, then these results carry no implications for the expected interbusiness-risk class risk-rate of return relationship. In fact their results are consistent with a positive relationship between leverage and rate of return over all firms.

Gale explicitly takes both leverage hypotheses into account by arguing that the principal determinant of interfirm variation in equity–asset ratios is business risk.[68] Gale's hypothesis is based on the assumption that there are optimal industry leverage rates with relatively small variations around them consistent with a negative rate of return–leverage relation within each industry, but that therefore the principal determinant of interindustry leverage differentials is industry-specific business risk. Gale tests the hypothesis on a sample of firms drawn from the largest in the manufacturing sector. The sampling procedure removes a potentially significant source of intraindustry variation in leverage because small firms are excluded. Business risk is assumed to derive solely from industry characteristics, like cyclical demand sensitivity and capital–output ratios required by production technologies, rather than from firm characteristics. For Gale's analysis as for that of Hall and Weiss, the relatively homogeneous large-firm sample group makes this a reasonable assumption. Gale's results are consistent with his hypothesis. The coefficient of leverage is positive even with concentration dummies in the equation. His hypothesis and results, however, carry the unlikely implication that the large, dominant, high-market-share firms which earn higher rates of return in his sample are riskier, in the business sense, than the smaller low-market-share firms, which earn lower rates of return.[69]

In summary, Gale interprets the positive interindustry leverage–rate of return relation as consistent with a tradeoff between business risk and return, while Caves, and Hall and

[68] Gale 1972.
[69] Large firms in a similar sample were found to have higher equity–assets ratios than small firms: Sullivan 1974, pp. 1407–14.

Weiss interpret the same result as indication that firms with significant market power can both earn above-average rates of return and experience below-average financial risk.

The core–periphery hypothesis, consistent with Gale and others, is that business risk, construed broadly to include the structural and behavioral impacts of membership in a particular industry, significantly affects firms' choice of capital structure and thus affects any interindustry analyses of the relation between leverage and rate of return. While Gale's argument that this results in a positive interindustry relation between leverage and rate of return is plausible within his relatively homogeneous sample of large firms, it is less so when a more heterogeneous population of firms is considered.

In a sample of core and periphery firms the significant differences in market power and competitive behavior are likely to affect the interindustry relation between leverage and rate of return. Although it is reasonable to assume that large firms in an industry respond in similar ways to industry conditions, the core–periphery hypothesis is that large firms and small firms within an industry experience industry conditions in very different ways and will thus respond to those conditions in different ways, including their choice of capital structure. As a result, intraindustry variation in leverage in a sample which includes core and periphery firms is likely to be as significant as interindustry variation. Therefore predictions about the relation between leverage and rate of return over the full sample are thrown into doubt.

Although Caves' hypothesis is structured in terms of the narrow financial-risk hypothesis, the question raised is an important one for a broader analysis of risk. Is it the case that firms with market power are systematically more risk-averse than other firms? Do firms with market power regularly choose a different point on the risk–return function than do firms without market power?

From the perspective of core and periphery, the answer is no. The question assumes that there is an underlying, immutable tradeoff between risk and rate of return which holds its functional form across all firms. Rather than choosing a different point on an underlying tradeoff, the core–periphery hypothesis is that core firms face a tradeoff with different terms as a result of their market power.[70] That core firms face a different tradeoff is quite different from suggesting that core firms use market power to "buy the tranquility of low leverage" (a higher ratio of equity to assets in Caves' usage). For example, it is hypothesized that the financial risk associated with any given degree of leverage in an industry is less for a core firm than for a periphery firm because of core firms' superior access to internal and external resources. In the same way, it is hypothesized that the business risk associated with membership in an industry is less for core than for periphery firms.

The samples used by Gale, and by Hall and Weiss mean that their results are relevant only to hypotheses about the relation between risk and return within the core. Their results are thus at least consistent with the core–periphery hypothesis about risk and return, which specifies business risk as a principal determinant of financial structure, but which also implies that there may be a different risk–return tradeoff within the periphery than within the core. A positive intracore or intraperiphery, interindustry leverage–rate of return relationship is consistent with the business-risk hypothesis. Similarly, a negative intracore or intraperiphery, intraindustry relationship is consistent with the hypothesis that financial risk is an independent determinant of profitability only within business-risk classes. However, there is no presumption in either case that the intracore and intraperiphery relationships are the same.

Cross-Sectional Profit Variability

Cross-sectional profit variability is a measure of the dispersion of profit rates among groups of firms defined by a variable like size or membership in an industry. Cross-sectional variability

[70] Hurdle 1974 also suggests that firms with market power may face a different tradeoff than firms without market power.

may provide some useful information about differentials in firm performance within groups of firms, but the actual connection of this measure to firm-specific risk is tenuous if it exists at all. Discussion of the cross-sectional variable is included in this section because it is generally dealt with in the literature under the heading of risk. Empirical studies have focussed on the relations between firm size or industry rates of return on one hand and cross-sectional risk measured by intrasize-class profit variability or intraindustry profit variability on the other.

Studies of the relation between size-class and intrasize-class profit variability have relatively uniform results; there is a consistent negative relation between the two.[71] As firms get larger they tend to earn profit rates significantly closer to their size-class mean than do smaller firms. This relation holds both for all corporations and for profitable firms alone.

The explanation provided for this pattern is similar to those proposed for the relation between size and time variability, that is, that large firm diversification makes them less susceptible to random influences.[72] At any particular time, small firms are more susceptible to both positive and negative noncyclical influences on profitability which result in a wider range of performance. It has been proposed that large diversified firms can be thought of as aggregations of n small independent operations, each equal in size to the mean size of firms in the smallest size group. In this case the variance of the profit rates for these large firms should be the inverse of the square root of n, times the variance of firms of size n. The data show that the variance of profit rates does decline with the size but that the actual variances for large firms are higher than the hypothetical variances.[73]

This explanation assumes that all individual business units are drawn from the same undifferentiated population, and

[71] Alexander 1949; Crum 1939; McConnell 1945; Samuels and Smyth 1968; Sherman 1968; Stekler 1963; Stekler 1964.
[72] Sherman 1968, pp. 117–20.
[73] Alexander 1949; Sherman 1968.

that these individual units are independent and subject to the same set of random influences. Thus, if some subunits are combined into groups of similar size (large firms) and the variance of the means of these groups (i.e., large-firm profit rates) is compared to the variance of the profit rates among non-grouped units, it follows in a purely statistical sense that the variance of the group means will be lower.

This view of diversification and large-firm structure is not consistent with the evidence as reviewed above. Large, dominant firms are not simply random samples of unrelated units and large firms have advantages more significant than the simple provision of an averaging function to a group of independent business subunits. Large firms tend to diversify in relatively small increments from positions of significant market power into related markets and when successful they extend their market dominance into these markets via the process of diversification. The fact that units of a large firm producing related products within a single industry may earn different rates of return does not mean that these units are like separate small firms. These units share a set of advantages that accrue to all parts of the larger firm, including financial and managerial resources, access to inputs, distribution networks, and shared advertising. It is clearly possible for large firms and small firms to be in the same industry and for the large firms to have larger market shares and to earn higher and less variable (in the cross-sectional sense) profit rates than the small firms. This difference in variability more plausibly reflects the market power of large firms, the fact that large firms are competing with one another across a full range of products, and the ability of large firms to transfer risk to smaller firms operating in relatively isolated niches than it reflects the purely statistical explanation.

It is also likely that some large firms operate in highly concentrated industries where they not only earn higher rates of profit than small firms within the industry but also earn higher rates of profit than small firms that face more intense intraindustry competition elsewhere. In fact, Sidney Alexander notes that small firms tend to be both in riskier industries and in riskier positions within industries.[74]

The fact that mean profit rates increase with firm size up to a point is also not consistent with the view that large firms are simply agglomerations of small firms drawn from the same population as the nongrouped small firms.[75] If the individual units are undifferentiated there is no reason to expect any systematic relation between group size and mean profit rate.

That the mean profit rate and the variance of profit rates level off at about the same size in the reported data is consistent with the core–periphery view that firms above some size tend to share the advantages of market power and therefore earn higher rates of return, and that interfirm competition within this group contributes to a similar mean level of return and thus reduced variation around that mean.[76]

The evidence then, is consistent with the core–periphery hypothesis about firm size and cross-sectional profit variability, that the active competition via diversification of core firms and the isolation of periphery firms in particular niches and in particular industries should result in lower cross-sectional variance for core firms than for periphery firms. This should appear, again given the weight of core firms in the population of large firms, as a negative relation between firm size and cross-sectional, in this case intrasize-class, variance. The hypothesis that small firms are more susceptible to noncyclical random influences is really a subpart of the more general core–periphery hypothesis that core firms' market power isolates them from various destabilizing influences and enables them to counteract others. It is hypothesized that core firms' maintenance of a more diversified product line both within and between industries is part of and a result of that market power and that the extension of core firms into new markets via diversification is essential to the maintenance of core firm status; that active

[74] Alexander 1949.
[75] Sherman 1968.
[76] Ibid.

process of diversification is a major contributor to the relative equality of profit rates among large firms.

The relation between industry rates of return and the variation of firm profit rates around the industry mean is also consistent across studies. The general finding is that there is a positive relation between industry average profitability and the variation of firm profit rates around that mean.[77]

The explanation in the literature for this positive association is frequently couched in terms of a risk–return tradeoff,[78] although there is relatively wide recognition that this cross-sectional measure does not capture the firm-specific risk–return relation very precisely, if at all. Another approach suggests that the intraindustry dispersion of profit rates represents the risk to a firm of entering that industry. If the risk is high, the expected profit rate must also be high in order to induce entry.[79]

This evidence is also consistent with the hypothesis that the intraindustry dispersion of profit rates is positively associated with domination by core firms and therefore positively associated with industry profit rates. In the core–periphery view, in core-dominated industries there is a core group and a periphery group with a significant difference in profitability between them and thus a relatively high intraindustry profit rate dispersion. The other polar structure in the core–periphery hypothesis is an industry composed primarily of periphery firms, which is expected to show comparatively more equal and lower profit rates because of stronger intraindustry competition. Insofar as the profit rates of core-dominated industries are heavily weighted toward high core-firm profit rates, the result will be the observed positive association between industry profitability and the intraindustry dispersion of profit rates.

Robert Stonebraker tested a closely related hypothesis, that the profitability of large firms in an industry is related posi-

---

[77] Cootner and Holland 1970; Conrad and Plotkin 1968; Winn 1975; Carleton and Silberman 1977.

[78] See, for example, Cootner and Holland 1970; Conrad and Plotkin 1968.

[79] Fisher and Hall 1969; Winn 1977.

tively to the risk of entry as indicated by the probability that a small firm entrant will earn less than the "competitive" rate of return.[80] His results suggest that small-firm risk, as measured by the performance of small-firm industry members, is significantly related to large-firm profitability. The results show no significant relation between large-firm profitability and the dispersion of large-firm profit rates.

Stonebraker's results are also consistent with the hypothesis advanced here. The significant positive correlation of large-firm profit rates with the probability that small firms will earn below-normal profits is predicted by the core–periphery model. In core-dominated industries it is expected that large firms will earn a high rate of return while periphery firms will face a higher probability of earning a lower than competitive rate of return. It is also expected, in the core–periphery hypothesis, that in industries not core-dominated, large firms with less market power will earn comparatively lower rates of return and periphery firms with a more favorable environment will have a higher probability of earning a profit rate equal to or greater than the competitive rate.

[80] Stonebraker 1976, pp. 33–39.

CHAPTER SIX

Empirical Tests of the Core–Periphery Hypotheses

THIS chapter presents empirical results from a series of tests designed to examine basic hypotheses of the core–periphery model as presented in chapter two. Briefly restated, the testable hypotheses are that core firms earn higher profit rates than do periphery firms; that there is less intragroup profit rate variability within the core than the periphery; and that core firms' profit rates are less risky than the profit rates of periphery firms.

The first step in assessing the empirical validity of the core–periphery hypotheses is a review of fourteen years of data on firm profitability and industry concentration levels drawn from the Internal Revenue Service (IRS) *Source Book of Statistics of Income*.[1] The advantage of these data is that they include information on firms over the full spectrum of firm size, unlike most data sets incorporating observations on individual firms, which are usually restricted to the top 500 to 1,000 firms in the economy.[2] Of the data most commonly used in cross-sectional industrial organization studies the IRS data are probably the most appropriate to the analysis of the core–periphery hypotheses. The principal drawback of the IRS data is that firms are grouped by asset-size class in each year. The result is that firm membership in each size class may vary over time as firms fail or change size classes, and that it is not possible to calculate the variance of profit rates within size groups. In addition the assignment of an entire firm's data to a single indus-

[1] U.S. Internal Revenue Service 1974.
[2] Typical data sets include the Fortune 500 or the approximately 1,200 firms on the Standard and Poor's Compustat tape.

try by the dominant industry method, and its resultant association with characteristics of that industry, tend to introduce significant amounts of statistical noise into estimates of structure–profitability relationships. The data, however, are adequate to provide some insight into general patterns and to provide a preliminary basis for support or rejection of the basic core–periphery hypotheses.

Table 1 derived from these data shows rates of profit by firm size and the level of industry concentration. A consistent pattern emerges from the annual data. Large firms in concentrated industries earn systematically higher profits than do all other firms, about 30 percent more than all other firms on average. The profit rates of all other firms fall fairly close together, although small firms in concentrated industries do better by a small margin than do small firms in less-concentrated industries or large firms in less-concentrated industries.

The evidence on the relative riskiness of core firm profits as

TABLE 1

Profit Rates by Firm Size and Industry Concentration

	small, low conc.	small, high conc.	large, low conc.	large, high conc.
1958	7.6	8.3	7.4	9.3
1959	9.5	10.6	9.5	12.4
1960	7.5	7.6	8.6	11.2
1961	7.3	7.3	8.0	10.4
1963	7.9	8.3	8.6	12.7
1964	8.9	9.0	8.6	12.4
1965	10.2	10.8	9.5	13.6
1966	10.9	12.3	10.1	12.2
1967	9.3	10.1	7.8	9.5
1968	9.2	10.8	7.3	13.7
1969	7.5	8.7	6.0	11.0
1970	5.4	4.9	5.0	5.7
1971	6.0	5.2	5.5	6.6
Average	8.2	8.8	7.8	10.8

SOURCE: U.S. Internal Revenue Service, various years, *Source Book of Statistics of Income.*

NOTE: Small size = less than $100 million in assets

Low concentration = four-firm concentration ratio less than 40.0

measured by temporal variability is somewhat less clear. The coefficients of relative variation over time show that the variability of core firms' profit rates was somewhat lower than that of the three periphery groups over the period 1958–1969 but that the pattern was reversed in the early 1970s. While this reversal may stem from substantive underlying causes any conclusion must await analysis of data more appropriate to the task. It is especially hazardous to use the IRS data for comparisons over long periods of time precisely because the actual firm membership in each subgroup may change significantly over time.

Analysis of the IRS data, at least through 1969, provides tentative support for the hypothesis that core firms earn higher profits than do periphery firms and that core firms' profit rates are less risky than those of periphery firms. These preliminary results from the best, easily available data on large and small firms, over a substantial period, provide the motivation for more detailed empirical analysis of a data set constructed for this study, which includes firm-level data on a sample of large and small firms.

The Sample

The basic data used in this study were drawn from four sources: 10-K reports filed annually by publicly traded corporations with the Securities and Exchange Commission (SEC); Standard and Poor's Compustat tape; the U.S. Internal Revenue Service *Source Book Statistics of Income*; and the U.S. Bureau of the Census *Enterprise Statistics*.[3]

Financial data on a sample of small manufacturing firms was collected from 10-K reports filed with the SEC. Four hundred small firms were selected randomly from the universe of all small publicly held firms that filed with the SEC in 1969. Of the 400 firms, 176 firms were excluded because of inade-

---

[3] U.S. Internal Revenue Service various years. U.S. Bureau of the Census, *Enterprise Statistics* various years.

quate data, illegible forms, or more than one year of missing data. Of the remaining 224 firms, 48 failed or were taken over between 1969 and 1973, and an additional 12 had missing data crucial to the analysis. The result was a sample of 154 firms, which existed continuously over the 1969 to 1973 period, and each of which had total assets in 1969 of less than $25 million.

Comparable financial data on a sample of larger manufacturing firms was collected from Standard and Poor's Compustat tape. The sample included all manufacturing firms with 1969 assets of greater than $25 million, or 572 firms.

Industry data at the IRS three-digit level of classification were drawn from a data set which included industry data from the Internal Revenue Service *Statistics of Income* and the LINK project of the Bureau of the Census.[4]

Firms were initially classified according to the SEC three-digit classification system, because in the case of small firms there was no other means of classification available. Large firms were classified the same way both for comparability with the small-firm method and because the Compustat industry classification system bears no discernible relation to any other system. Subsequently the industry classification systems of the SEC and the IRS were adjusted for compatibility. The result was that firms were classified in one of fifty-seven three-digit nondefense manufacturing industries, which correspond closely to the 1976 SEC classification system.

THE VARIABLES

The profit rate is a central variable in the empirical tests of this study. There are a number of issues related to the appropriate measure of the profit rate and a variety of biases that affect the profit rate regardless of the specific measure.

A basic theorem of neoclassical economics holds that in the long run risk-adjusted rates of profit tend to be equalized

[4] U.S. Bureau of the Census, *Enterprise Statistics* various years.

across industries by the force of competition, given relatively free capital mobility. From the perspective of the core–periphery analysis that profit rate can only be the profit rate on investment, or equivalently, the profit rate on total assets if measures are limited to available accounting data.

Some analysts argue that there are measures of profitability theoretically superior to such accounting-based measures.[5] As Thomas Stauffer's work has indicated, however, the adjustments required to calculate such rates of return are cumbersome and the actual gains are doubtful; there is a high correlation between accounting rates of return and adjusted rates of return for the sample of industries studied.[6] On a more pragmatic level the present analysis addresses theoretical and empirical issues raised within the industrial organization tradition. Comparisons with the empirical results of that literature would clearly not be meaningful if a conceptually different profit rate measure were used.[7]

Alternative accounting measures of the profit rate include principally return on equity and return on total assets. The argument for return on equity, briefly, is that managers maximize the stockholders' interest, which can best be defined by the rate of return on stockholders' equity, or net worth.[8] However, this measure gives an undue importance to firm financial structure in that firms with a large proportion of debt will show higher rates of return than firms with equivalent rates of return on assets but larger proportions of equity in their capital structure. This financial structure is determined by a variety of other forces. As Bradley Gale points out, an equal rate of return on equity would "imply a world of too many resources earning a low rate of return on assets in industries with low percentages of equity capital, and too few resources earning a

---

[5] Stauffer 1971a; Stauffer 1971b; Fisher and McGowan 1983; Fisher 1984.

[6] Stauffer 1971a; Stauffer 1971b.

[7] For other defenses of accounting-based profit measures, see Horowitz 1984; Long and Ravenscraft 1984; Van Breda 1984.

[8] See, for example, Hall and Weiss 1967.

high rate of return on assets in industries with high percentages of equity capital."[9]

The rate of profit is measured here as the ratio of net income to total assets. This is a traditional measure used to evaluate firm performance.[10] In addition, as a check on the results, the analysis is performed with rate of return on equity as a profit measure, where the return on equity is the ratio of net income to the book value of stockholders' equity.[11]

An important bias is introduced into measured rates of return by traditional methods of asset valuation in the presence of inflation. Firms with newer assets purchased at higher prices will tend to have a lower measured profit rate than firms with older assets, embodying comparable technology, valued at their lower purchase price. The problem is mitigated to the extent that higher prices paid for new assets reflect technological advance rather than pure inflation.[12] The result can overstate the profit rates of firms which are growing slowly relative to

[9] Gale 1972.

[10] Brigham 1977, pp. 179–85; Carleton and Silberman 1977.

[11] Industrial organization economists frequently use an overall rate of return measure, which includes net income and interest payments in the numerator and total assets in the denominator, in structure-performance tests like those presented in this study (Scherer 1980, pp. 268-69). However, it is not clear that the overall return measure with interest payments included is conceptually superior to a measure that excludes interest payments. The former overall return measure includes net income, which is income net of interest payments and taxes, plus interest payments. The implicit rationale is that net income represents the earnings associated with equity while interest payments represent the earnings associated with debt. The problem arises in that total interest payments do not reflect, from the firm's perspective, the earnings explicitly associated with the debt component of capitalization because they ignore the tax effect of debt. Interest payments net of taxes represent the cost of debt to the firm and the tax benefits flow to net income. When total interest payments are used, the tax benefit is imputed to debt as well as explicitly included in net income. This suggests that total assets are a reasonable denominator to use with net income from the perspective of matching earnings with assets, because a portion of net income is the tax savings associated with the use of debt. From the firm's perspective these earnings are the direct result of the use of debt.

[12] Scherer 1980, p. 272.

firms which are growing rapidly. Since high-growth firms are likely to have higher profit rates, the bias is toward equal measured profit rates across firms. Since there is in general only a weak relation between industry concentration levels and firm growth, there will not be systematic bias introduced into the concentration–profitability relation. If there is a relatively strong positive correlation between firm growth rates and firm size then this asset valuation problem will create a bias toward lower large-firm profit rates, higher small-firm profit rates, and thus a reduced differential between core and periphery firms.

A second issue related to asset valuation is that assets belonging to firms that are purchased and merged into existing companies are likely to be revalued upward to capitalize expected earnings. Thus the assets of firms with a larger proportion of assets acquired through merger will, *ceteris paribus*, tend to have lower measured profit rates than other firms.[13] Since large dominant firms have a higher proportion of merged assets than small firms, the bias is again toward a reduced core–periphery differential.

A final and perhaps the most important bias affecting interfirm comparisons of profitability derives from the sample selection process. The Compustat data set is a retrospective sample in that it includes historical data only for firms that existed at the time the tape was compiled. This attribute derives from the principal use of these data, which is investment analysis; not many analysts are interested in firms which have failed. In order to make the small and large firm data sets comparable the small firm data was assembled in the same way. Only firms which survived over the full five-year period are included in the data. The resulting bias is similar to that which follows from the exclusion of nonpositive profit firms in analyses of firm size and profitability. In that case the result is to reverse the relation between size and profitability. Although the effect should not be as marked in this case, the exclusion of firms which failed over the period biases the size–profitability relation toward the

[13] Ibid.

negative because a much larger proportion of small firms fail than large firms and because low and/or negative profits are generally associated with firm failure.

Another principal variable in the analysis is the four-firm concentration ratio, which is the proportion of sales in an industry contributed by the top four firms. There are several well-known problems with simple concentration ratios, yet, there is no general agreement that a better measure of joint firm dominance exists. The major problems with concentration ratios are that they do not conform well with more precise definitions of markets, and they do not take into account geographical submarkets, noncompeting products within industries, interindustry competition from products classified in another industry, or international competition.[14]

These problems take on a somewhat different cast from the perspective of core and periphery. The traditional definition of a market depends on the notion of homogeneous or closely related products. At the simplest level, a single product defines a market. Substitute goods, in a relatively narrow sense, can also be part of an industry, although broadly defined substitutes, such as various forms of transportation, often fall into different industries.[15] However, as detailed in chapter two, variation in the mix of products offered within an "industry" constitutes a basic element of core firms' competitive tactics. Industries, in a sense, are defined by the firms which dominate them. If large firms in an industry produce a broad line of goods while periphery firms produce varying parts of that broad line, is the relevant definition of industry all products produced by the core firms or the subportions of the product line produced by groups of periphery firms?

These considerations make the use of certain industry data at the fairly broad three-digit level more acceptable for this study than it is for more traditionally conceived studies. The fact that all of the financial data associated with a firm is

[14] Shepherd 1970; Weiss 1963; Weiss 1972.
[15] See, for example, Scherer 1980, pp. 56–64.

lumped into a single industry risks contamination of the data when the firm is significantly diversified across three-digit industries. The use of the three-digit classification reduces this problem compared to use of four-digit industries, but some such data contamination is unavoidable and undoubtedly present in this study.

Nonetheless, the market power of core firms may in fact be represented best by the concentration ratios in the relatively narrowly defined industries which make up a core firm's home industry. It is frequently in a narrowly defined home industry that core firms have a mature core position from which their capacity to invest elsewhere and establish new core positions is derived. Measuring core firms' market power over too broad a line of goods tends to understate their real market power and thus bias the concentration/size–profitability relation toward zero. If concentration is to be the market power proxy, the weighted averages of concentration within relatively narrowly defined (four-digit) industries are probably the most appropriate for market power–rate of return tests. Core firms' diversified positions are frequently "transitional" in that they have not yet fully established market power in the new markets. This tends to bias downwards their overall profit rate and to reduce the significance of the concentration–profitability correlation.

While neither the four-digit nor the three-digit level of analysis is ideal, this study uses a combination of the two (which unfortunately cannot be said to combine the best properties of each). The best method would have been to obtain appropriate constituent four-digit concentration ratios for each firm. However, it was not possible to classify each firm into one or more four-digit industries. Adequate data to so classify the small firms in the sample did not exist in an accessible form. Firms were classified according to the SEC's three-digit classification system. The compatible industry data, which were drawn from the combined IRS-Census LINK project data, contained concentration ratios obtained from constituent four-digit industries via a weighting process. The four-digit-level concentration ratios were obtained from the Census of Manufactures and were not considered to adequately reflect concentration levels due to the well-documented problems cited above.[16] The method used here was to substitute William Shepherd's corrected four-digit concentration ratios, to weight them by the value of shipments, and to calculate on that basis a weighted average three-digit concentration ratio compatible with SEC industry classifications.[17]

The concentration ratios which resulted from this procedure, while the best available for this study, still suffer from substantial drawbacks. Most important is that at the relatively broad three-digit level, concentration ratios simply cannot reflect the realities of market structure and relative market power very accurately. Unfortunately the bias in the three-digit-level concentration ratios is probably not systematically in one direction. Since three-digit industries consist of four-digit industries with frequently wide variations in levels of concentration, the resultant weighted-average three-digit concentration ratio will show less variation, and variation that reflects less accurately the actual market conditions of any particular firm. The result will be to provide a relatively strong bias toward a nonsignificant relationship of any kind between concentration and firm profitability.

The remaining firm variables are less controversial. Size is measured as total assets where total assets are as reported on a firm's balance sheet and consist principally of total current assets, net fixed assets, and total other assets. The temporal standard deviation of profitability is exactly that measured over the full five-year period.[18] Leverage is defined as the ratio of total equity to total assets.

[16] U.S. Bureau of the Census, *Enterprise Statistics* various years.
[17] U.S. Bureau of the Census 1971.
[18] Temporal standard deviation is measured as:

$$TSD = \left[\sum_{t=69}^{73} \frac{(PRFT_{it} - MPRFT_i)^2}{5} \right]^{1/2}$$

The industry variables are available in each case only for the three-year period 1969 to 1971. The capital–output ratio is the ratio of industry total assets to industry net sales. The industry growth rate is measured as the ratio of the overall increase in sales to the first-year sales. The firm growth rate is also measured as the ratio of the overall increase in sales to the first-year sales and the difference in the two rates is calculated by simple subtraction.

EMPIRICAL RESULTS

The central empirical hypothesis of this study is that core firms earn higher and less risky profit rates with lower intragroup variation than do periphery firms. The core–periphery hypothesis implies the existence of size and concentration thresholds which define the boundaries of core and periphery groups. In order directly to test this hypothesis and the related subhypotheses detailed in chapter two it must be determined whether the thresholds exist, and the actual levels of the thresholds.

The theory of core and periphery suggests that large firms gain a greater advantage from high levels of concentration than do small firms. The hypothesis tested first will be that there is some firm size, above which concentration has a positive effect on profitability and below which it does not. The review of the empirical literature in chapter five suggests that concentration may have a negative effect on profitability for small firms and a positive effect for large firms.

In order to test this hypothesis, the size above which concentration has its maximum effect on profitability must be determined. If it is the case that concentration has a positive, significant effect only above some firm size, then this procedure will select that size.[19]

[19] There may be a tendency for this test to underestimate the correct size threshold if, as is the case here, both the mean profit level and mean concentration level are significantly lower for relatively small firms than for larger

The model used to test this hypothesis is the following:

$$\text{PRFT} = a + b_1\text{CONC} + b_2(1/\text{SIZE}) + b_3\text{TSD} + b_4\text{LVG} + b_5\text{GRDA} + b_6\text{GRI} + b_7\text{KAPO}$$

PRFT: profit rate by firm
CONC: four-firm concentration ratio
SIZE: firm asset size
TSD: temporal standard deviation of firm profit rate
LVG: leverage, or the ratio of equity to assets, by firm
GRDA: difference between firm sales growth and industry
      sales growth
GRI: industry sales growth
KAPO: industry capital–output ratio

In order to determine this size threshold the regression model was tested over subsets of the data defined by firm size. For each size threshold the model was tested separately for all firms larger than that size and for all firms smaller than that size.

That size, above which the regression coefficient of the concentration variable is maximized, is considered the critical size threshold. In 1969, 1970, 1971, and 1973 that size is $80M in assets, measured in 1969. In 1972 it is $60M. The results also suggest that where concentration has a significant effect for relatively small firms, that effect is restricted to firms below $20M in asset size. As an additional test, therefore, the regression model was estimated for firms between asset sizes of $20M and $80M, between $20M and $90M, and between $20M and $100M. Concentration has a nonsignificant coefficient between $20M and $80M in every year, but the coefficient becomes positive and significant in every year when firms of asset size greater than $80M are included.

Taken together these results suggest a consistent pattern across all five years. In every year, concentration has a positive, significant effect on profitability only for firms larger than

firms. The additional tests used below provide a check on this tendency, which appears to be a problem only in 1972.

$80M in assets. Concentration has a relatively strong effect for firms below $80M only below a relatively small size, about $20M in assets. For firms which fall between that lower size and the $80M threshold, however, there is no significant profitability–concentration relationship in any year. In effect, there is a buffer group between small firms and large firms. Table 2 presents the regression results for the model estimated separately for firms greater than and for firms less than $80M in size.

For each year the Chow-F statistic was calculated for each pair of regressions. These statistics are: 1969–3.49; 1970–4.43; 1971–2.93; 1972–2.30; 1973–3.20. The critical value of the F statistic at the .05 level of significance is 1.94. Thus in each year the regressions above and below the size threshold exhibit significantly different structures. Further, in every year the mean profit rate of all firms above the size threshold is significantly greater than that for all firms below the size threshold.

The regression results suggest a more complex pattern of profitability–size–concentration interaction than originally thought, but nonetheless one that is consistent with the core–periphery hypothesis. Although it is not true that concentration has a uniformly negative effect on the profit rates of small firms, it does have a negative, nonsignificant effect for firms smaller than $20M in 1969, 1971, and 1972. There is a nonsignificant, positive relationship for similarly small firms in 1970 and 1973.[20]

To summarize, the regression results reported are consistent with the hypothesis that in every year there is a size threshold above which firms gain significant increases in profitability from increased levels of industry concentration, and below

[20] It is worth noting that the core–periphery hypothesis does not require that the coefficients of the concentration variable be significantly different between large and small firms. They are significantly different in 1969, 1971, and 1972. All that is required at this point is that there be a positive coefficient for large firms and that the mean profit rate of large firms be higher than that of small firms. Both are true in every year.

TABLE 2

Regressions by Size Threshold

(Standard Errors in Parentheses)

PRFT =	a	+	b₁CONC	+	b₂(1/SIZE)	+	b₃TSD	+	b₄LVG	+	b₅GRI	+	b₆GRDA	+	b₇KAPO	R²
Above Threshold																
1969	-.051		.00046 (.00009)		212.309 (410.887)		-.120 (.118)		.185 (.010)		.022 (.011)		.010 (.003)		-.026 (.007)	.47
1970	-.047		.00036 (.00010)		-162.716 (460.859)		-.664 (.126)		.181 (.011)		.028 (.012)		.015 (.004)		-.023 (.007)	.50
1971	-.046		.00054 (.00009)		471.025 (434.828)		-1.208 (.118)		.176 (.010)		.043 (.011)		.021 (.003)		-.035 (.006)	.62
1972	-.047		.00048 (.00010)		593.349 (468.631)		-.340 (.124)		.172 (.010)		.037 (.011)		.017 (.004)		-.029 (.006)	.52
1973	-.043		.00030 (.00009)		-122.571 (442.700)		.412 (.111)		.171 (.009)		.039 (.010)		.019 (.003)		-.018 (.005)	.50
Below Threshold																
1969	-.016		-.00045 (.00026)		-37.444 (20.520)		-.646 (.090)		.190 (.020)		.043 (.029)		.017 (.006)		-.003 (.020)	.45
1970	-.006		.00016 (.00029)		-3.725 (23.073)		-1.628 (.106)		.140 (.022)		.064 (.032)		.033 (.006)		-.024 (.019)	.65
1971	-.035		-.00038 (.00027)		-.353 (21.541)		-1.154 (.109)		.188 (.020)		.108 (.030)		.041 (.006)		-.007 (.017)	.66
1972	-.037		-.00037 (.00027)		-.011 (23.598)		-.529 (.106)		.183 (.020)		.078 (.031)		.025 (.006)		-.002 (.017)	.44
1973	-.023		.00047 (.00027)		-135.705 (23.867)		-.339 (.108)		.135 (.019)		-.030 (.030)		.030 (.006)		-.015 (.017)	.46

which firms do not consistently gain from increased concentration.

The nature of the relationship between levels of concentration and profitability for firms above the size threshold remains to be determined. The hypothesis derived from the core–periphery analysis is that there is a threshold level of concentration above which large firms earn a rate of return higher than that earned by large firms in industries with concentration levels below that threshold, and, by extension, higher than that earned by all firms below the size threshold as well.

The second hypothesis is tested using the following model:

$$\text{PRFT} = a + b_1\text{CR}_1 + b_2(1/\text{SIZE}) + b_3\text{TSD} + b_4\text{LVG} + b_5\text{GRDA} + b_6\text{GRI} + b_7\text{KAPO}$$

CR_1: concentration dummy

In this model concentration is represented by a dummy variable that equals one when the concentration ratio is above some level and zero if the concentration ratio is below that level.

The model was estimated over the full range of concentration levels represented in the data. The level which maximizes the coefficient of the concentration dummy variable is the level at which there is the largest difference in profitability between the high-concentration group and the low-concentration group. This level is an estimate of the threshold concentration ratio which separates large, core firms from large, periphery firms. The regression results show that the threshold level of concentration varies somewhat by year but that it has a positive significant coefficient in each year. The critical concentration levels are: 1969–59.0; 1970–61.0; 1971–63.0; 1972–59.0; 1973–59.0. The estimated regression equations are presented in Table 3.[21]

[21] The estimates of the concentration threshold are comparable to estimates in the literature of a critical concentration ratio. In general, these estimates have been made on a data set consisting solely of large firms. The estimates here, which range from a four-firm concentration ratio of 59.0 to 63.0, depending on the year, are relatively close to previous estimates, which range from 50.0 to 59.0.

TABLE 3
Concentration Threshold Regressions
(Standard Errors in Parentheses)

PRFT =	a	+ b_1CR1	+ b_2(1/SIZE)	+ b_3TSD	+ b_4LVG	+ b_5GRI	+ b_6GRDA	+ b_7KAPO	R^2
1969	−.030	.018 (.003)	163.419 (405.308)	−.150 (.117)	.190 (.010)	.020 (.011)	.011 (.003)	−.032 (.007)	.48
1970	−.032	.013 (.003)	−161.594 (458.594)	−.627 (.125)	.184 (.011)	.029 (.012)	.015 (.004)	−.026 (.007)	.50
1971	−.023	.016 (.003)	393.292 (439.029)	−1.165 (.118)	.180 (.010)	.044 (.011)	.021 (.003)	−.034 (.006)	.62
1972	−.026	.018 (.003)	486.611 (460.514)	−.351 (.123)	.176 (.010)	.035 (.011)	.018 (.004)	−.034 (.006)	.53
1973	−.030	.012 (.003)	−158.892 (436.920)	.400 (.111)	.174 (.009)	.038 (.010)	.020 (.003)	−.021 (.006)	.51

NOTE. The regressions include CR1 at the concentration threshold level only. The concentration thresholds for each year are: 1969–59.0; 1970–61.0; 1971–63.0; 1972–59.0; 1973–59.0.

In order to establish the existence of a concentration threshold it must also be determined whether concentration has an independent continuous effect on profitability for large firms either above or below the concentration threshold. Equations were estimated for each group of firms for each year with concentration included as a continuous variable. The results show that for large firms below the concentration threshold, concentration has no significant effect on profitability in any year. Likewise for large firms above the concentration threshold, concentration has no significant effect on profitability in four of five years. In 1971 the concentration variable has a positive significant effect for this group of firms.

The Chow-F statistic was also calculated for each pair of equations. The values of these statistics are: 1969–9.31; 1970–4.62; 1971–6.85; 1972–9.95; 1973–5.37. The critical value of F at the .01 level of significance is 2.51. Thus in each year the regression equations for all large firms above the concentration threshold are significantly different than the regression equations for all large firms below the concentration threshold.

These results establish the existence of a concentration threshold for large firms. Together with the size threshold established earlier, the joint size–concentration threshold delimiting core and periphery groups has been established. All firms larger than the size threshold and in industries with concentration levels above the concentration threshold are defined to be core firms and all other firms are periphery firms.

The critical test of the core–periphery hypothesis is the comparison of profit rates by core and periphery groups. Table 4 shows the profit rates by year for firms in the core and periphery groups. In every year the profit rate for the core group is higher than the profit rate for the periphery group. The difference between these mean profit rates is highly significant in each year. Core firm profit rates are higher than periphery firm

---

See, for example, Bain 1951; Meehan and Duchesneau 1973; Rhoades and Cleaver 1973; White 1976.

TABLE 4
Core–Periphery Means

	Core			Periphery		
	PRFT	TSD	LVG	PRFT	TSD	LVG
1969	.0657	.0139	.5458	.0525	.0251	.5655
1970	.0537	.0128	.5341	.0339	.0249	.5518
1971	.0520	.0131	.5327	.0365	.0243	.5514
1972	.0582	.0139	.5251	.0458	.0251	.5500
1973	.0661	.0139	.5103	.0528	.0251	.5259

profit rates by an average of 35 percent. The range is from 25 percent higher in 1969 to 58 percent higher in 1970.

An additional test is the comparison of regression equations for core and periphery groups. The following equation was estimated for each group of firms:

$$\text{PRFT} = a + b_1(1/\text{SIZE}) + b_2\text{TSD} + b_3\text{LVG} + b_4\text{GRDA} + b_5\text{GRI} + b_6\text{KAPO}$$

The results are reported in Table 5. The Chow-F statistic was calculated for each pair of equations. These statistics are: 1969–3.99; 1970–3.25; 1971–2.05; 1972–4.07; 1973–3.05. In each of the five years the statistic is significant at the .05 level of significance. The critical value of F is 2.01.

It is worth commenting at this point on the meaning of the Chow test for the core–periphery hypothesis. The Chow test indicates the structural similarity or differences between estimates of a regression model over two parts of a data set. The Chow test allows an answer to the question of whether the same regression equation holds in an additional part of the data set as held in the first part.

While it is of interest whether the same regression relation holds within the core as within the periphery group, an affirmative answer is not essential to the basic hypothesis of different mean profit rates between core and periphery. In effect the regression equations are used to define the core by establishing threshold levels of firm size and industry concentration, but

TABLE 5
Core–Periphery Regressions
(Standard Errors in Parentheses)

PRFT =	a	+	b_1(1/SIZE)	+	$b_{2,TSD}$	+	$b_{3,LVG}$	+	$b_{4,GRI}$	+	$b_{5,GRDA}$	+	$b_{6,KAPO}$	R^2
Core														
1969	-.018		519.082 (573.822)		-.013 (.142)		.218 (.015)		.022 (.017)		.018 (.006)		-.048 (.009)	.56
1970	-.037		540.068 (744.793)		-.569 (.212)		.217 (.018)		.023 (.019)		.019 (.007)		-.029 (.010)	.52
1971	-.025		724.327 (688.038)		-.643 (.182)		.198 (.015)		.046 (.016)		.025 (.006)		-.036 (.008)	.63
1972	-.005		1608.867 (656.193)		-.135 (.150)		.176 (.014)		.037 (.017)		.019 (.006)		-.044 (.008)	.55
1973	-.014		1027.822 (636.678)		.399 (.135)		.173 (.013)		.037 (.015)		.028 (.005)		-.031 (.008)	.53
Periphery														
1969	-.027		-31.568 (16.204)		-.639 (.071)		.180 (.014)		.027 (.017)		.013 (.004)		-.015 (.011)	.44
1970	-.013		-1.418 (17.788)		-1.557 (.080)		.144 (.015)		.057 (.019)		.027 (.004)		-.010 (.010)	.63
1971	-.039		1.772 (16.508)		-1.180 (.080)		.182 (.013)		.081 (.017)		.035 (.004)		-.020 (.009)	.65
1972	-.041		-2.418 (18.473)		-.553 (.082)		.179 (.014)		.060 (.018)		.023 (.004)		-.014 (.009)	.46
1973	-.025		-132.828 (18.911)		-.284 (.084)		.147 (.014)		.016 (.018)		.026 (.004)		.004 (.009)	.45

they are explicitly not used in such a way as to maximize the overall structural difference between the regression equations. That is not theoretically appropriate in this case and thus is not the empirical methodology employed.[22]

The intent of this analysis is different. The coefficient on concentration is the sole criterion in establishing the size threshold because the focus of the analysis is on the interaction between size, concentration, and profitability. A single equation with a dummy variable for concentration is used in establishing the concentration threshold because the intent is to maximize differences in profitability by concentration category and not to maximize the overall differences between the equations.

To maximize the overall differences between equations would accord equal potential significance to each of the independent variables in defining core and periphery. That is not appropriate because the theory defines core and periphery by levels of size and concentration alone. While it is appropriate to include other independent variables in the regression equations used to estimate the boundaries of the core, the coefficients on those variables are of interest only within the core and periphery groups.

It is expected that the variance of profit rates within the group of core firms will be significantly less than the variance of profit rates within the periphery group as a result of different patterns of competition within the two groups. Since the ratio of the sample variances is distributed as an F distribution (under the null hypothesis that there is no difference in variances), the test of this hypothesis requires comparison of the two sample variances taking into account degrees of freedom.[23]

Table 6 presents the sample variances by year for core and periphery firm profit rates. The value of the ratio of the sample

[22] See White 1976 for a good example of how such a methodology can be implemented. Chow 1960.

[23] Kmenta 1971, pp. 147–48.

TABLE 6

Cross-Sectional Variance of Profit Rates

	(1) core sample variance	(2) periphery sample variance	(3) (2)/(1)
1969	.0019	.0041	2.16
1970	.0021	.0077	3.67
1971	.0018	.0071	3.94
1972	.0018	.0048	2.67
1973	.0015	.0047	3.13

$F_{.01, 120, 120} = 1.53$

variances is significant for each year and supports the hypothesis that core cross-sectional profit variation is significantly lower than that within the periphery.

There are two measures of risk incorporated in the estimated regressions and the results for each are somewhat different. The first measure is the temporal standard deviation of profit rates (TSD). The results show that risk as measured by the mean value of the TSD variable is lower for the core group than for the periphery group and that the difference is statistically significant for each of the slightly different core thresholds. (See Table 4.)

Effectively, then, there is a negative intergroup relationship between profit rates and the temporal risk measure. The mean profit rate is higher for core firms than for periphery firms while temporal risk is lower for core firms. This reverses the expected positive tradeoff between temporal risk and profit rates. Core firms combine the positive attributes of high profit rates and low temporal risk.

Another facet of the risk–profitability relationship involves the coefficient of the risk variable in the regression equations estimated separately for core and periphery firms. Given that the level of risk is lower among core firms, this coefficient describes the relationship between risk and profitability within each group. (See Table 5.)

The coefficients of the risk variable are negative and significant for periphery firms in every year while the core group risk coefficient is negative but nonsignificant in 1969 and 1972, is positive and significant in 1973 and is negative and significant in 1970 and 1971. Thus the intragroup relationship between profit rates and the temporal risk measure is also generally negative. Firms within core and periphery groups, respectively, that have higher profit rates than other group members tend also to have lower temporal risk. In addition, the coefficient for periphery firms is more negative than that for core firms in every year. This difference is statistically significant in each year. The combination of lower levels of temporal risk and higher profit levels summarizes the superior risk–return performance of core firms.

The other measure of risk employed in this analysis is leverage, measured by the ratio of equity to total assets. The results of the profit–risk tradeoff using the leverage measure are consistent with the analysis of results with the temporal measure. The mean level of leverage in the core is significantly lower than that in the periphery. (See Table 4.) Effectively there is a negative intergroup relationship between the profit rate and leverage; the mean profit rate is higher for core firms than for periphery firms while the leverage ratio is lower for core firms.

This result is consistent with the theoretical expectation outlined in chapter five about the relationship between business risk and financial risk. Core firms, as a result of superior market power, are hypothesized to have lower business risk on average than do periphery firms. It is expected that as a result core firms would maintain a lower leverage ratio than periphery firms. Periphery firms facing higher business risk would attempt to offset that risk, in part, with lower financial risk and thus a higher leverage ratio.

Another aspect of the profit–risk relationship with the financial risk measure involves the nature of that relationship within the core and periphery groups. The coefficients of the leverage variable in the regressions estimated for core and for periphery firms are positive and significant in both cases. (See

Table 5.) Further, they are very close in value and are not statistically significantly different. This result is also consistent with the hypothesis of chapter five that while there is a different tradeoff among core firms than among periphery firms (in the sense that mean profit rates and degrees of leverage are significantly different), that the business risk hypothesis is supported within core and periphery groups.

Insofar as higher business risk induces firms to choose a less risky financial structure, that is, higher leverage, a positive relationship is expected between profit and leverage, which would reflect a profit–risk tradeoff. As suggested in chapter five, this positive relationship within core and periphery groups is consistent with an intragroup tradeoff which is reversed between core and periphery groups as a result of core firms' market power.

Firm size is represented as the reciprocal of firm asset size, consistent with results on the shape of the relationship between size and profitability in the literature cited in chapter five. In regression results for all firms in the data set, size has a significant, positive effect on profitability. The reciprocal form implies a decreasing slope as size increases. This flattening of the profit–size relation occurred between firm sizes of from approximately $40 to $100 million in assets, measured in 1969.

In the regression equations for core and periphery reported in Table 5 the coefficients on size are affected by collinearity with the temporal risk measure and their meaning in these regressions is somewhat suspect. There is no indication that this affected the threshold estimates; these estimates are almost identical with those estimated via regressions without the temporal risk measure. In regressions without TSD the effect of size is as expected from the shape of the overall profit–size relationship: positive and significant for periphery firms and nonsignificant for core firms.

The coefficients of the industry growth variable are positive and significant in three of five years for core firms. For periphery firms the coefficients are also positive and significant in three of five years. The results suggest that variations in industry growth rates affect core and periphery firm profitability about equally. However, the mean industry growth rate for core firms is significantly higher than that for periphery firms: 3.13 percent annually for core firms and 1.92 percent for periphery firms. The industries dominated by core firms grew on average at a faster rate than did those populated primarily by periphery firms.

The coefficients of the variable measuring the differential between firm and industry growth are positive and significant in every year for both core and periphery firms. These results suggest that variations in the firm–industry growth differential also affect core and periphery firm profit rates about equally. The mean firm–industry growth differential for core firms is significantly lower than that for periphery firms. While the industries dominated by core firms grew more rapidly than the industries of periphery firms, firm growth tended to match industry growth more closely for core than for periphery firms.

The industry capital–output ratio has a significant negative effect on core firm profit rates in each sample year while it has no significant effect on periphery firm profit rates in any year except 1971, where it has a negative, significant effect. At the same time, mean levels of the capital–output ratio are significantly higher for core than for periphery firms. Within the core group, relatively high levels of industry capital–output ratio are associated with lower levels of profitability, but the core group overall combines a higher mean profit rate with a higher mean capital–output ratio. This finding is consistent with the existence of capital barriers to core-dominated industry entry, which contribute to core–periphery performance differentials, but also suggests that within the core group, location in relatively more capital-intensive industries has a negative effect on profitability.

In an effort to ascertain the sensitivity of the results to the profit measure, the analysis was repeated with the rate of return on equity as the dependent variable. The general results on the relationship of core to periphery profitability and risk with the return on equity measure are identical to those with the overall rate of return measure, although there are some differences in other areas. (See Table 7.)

The existence of size and concentration thresholds is confirmed with the return on equity measure, although the size thresholds are somewhat different and show slightly more year-to-year variation than with the overall rate of return measure. The size thresholds are: 1969–$50M in 1969 assets; 1970–$60M; 1971–$60M; 1972–$80M; 1973–$110M. The concentration thresholds are: 1969–61.0; 1970–59.0; 1971–61.0; 1972–59.0; 1973–59.0.

In every year the rate of return on equity is significantly higher for core than for periphery firms. Core firm rates of return on equity are higher than periphery firm rates of return by an average of 80 percent. The range is from 34 percent higher in 1969 to 120 percent in 1970.

The regression equations estimated above for core and periphery groups are reestimated with return on equity as the dependent variable. The results are presented in Table 8. Again, the Chow-F statistic was calculated for each pair of equations. These statistics are: 1969–1.22; 1970–3.27; 1971–1.11; 1972–3.52; 1973–3.45. The statistic is significant at the .01 level in 1970, 1972, and 1973 and not significant in 1969 and 1971. As discussed above, while these results suggest that the regression relations are significantly different between core and periphery in three years and not significantly different in

TABLE 7

Core–Periphery Means
(Return on Equity)

	Core			Periphery		
	Profit	TSD	LVG	Profit	TSD	LVG
1969	.1151	.0309	.5473	.0859	.0725	.5685
1970	.0846	.0360	.5326	.0385	.0717	.5585
1971	.0850	.0312	.5350	.0444	.0714	.5585
1972	.1018	.0362	.5284	.0519	.0700	.5552
1973	.1224	.0331	.5119	.0776	.0694	.5322

TABLE 8

Core–Periphery Regressions
(Return on Equity)
(Standard Errors in Parentheses)

PRFT =	a	+	b_1(1/SIZE)	+	b_2TSD	+	b_3LVG	+	b_4GRI	+	b_5GRDA	+	b_6KAPO	R^2
						Core								
1969	.092		979.395 (713.778)		-.402 (.068)		.172 (.031)		.040 (.031)		.013 (.011)		-.074 (.017)	.35
1970	.013		-2348.933 (1246.497)		-.483 (.069)		.262 (.041)		-.003 (.045)		.014 (.015)		-.044 (.021)	.38
1971	.042		440.369 (952.406)		-.955 (.068)		.196 (.030)		.086 (.030)		.027 (.011)		-.051 (.014)	.67
1972	.120		3571.609 (2463.107)		-.384 (.099)		.105 (.060)		.077 (.060)		.001 (.021)		-.079 (.030)	.17
1973	.097		-3941.564 (1505.486)		.131 (.044)		.106 (.028)		.090 (.026)		.051 (.009)		-.053 (.013)	.30
						Periphery								
1969	.014		-113.627 (50.216)		-.236 (.036)		.197 (.049)		-.019 (.059)		.031 (.013)		-.038 (.039)	.18
1970	.078		-4.504 (66.109)		-1.082 (.050)		.132 (.065)		.211 (.078)		.025 (.018)		-.074 (.043)	.59
1971	-.077		-14.310 (67.143)		-.592 (.051)		.254 (.063)		.113 (.076)		.085 (.017)		-.028 (.040)	.37
1972	.049		-149.415 (80.221)		-1.093 (.584)		.120 (.073)		.120 (.086)		.038 (.020)		-.002 (.043)	.53
1973	.182		-70.968 (101.311)		-1.144 (.074)		-.027 (.092)		.186 (.108)		.043 (.026)		-.045 (.052)	.40

two years, this result does not bear directly on the basic core–periphery hypothesis.

Table 9 presents the sample variances by year for core and periphery firm profit rates. The value of the ratio of the sample variances is significant for each year and further supports the hypothesis that core cross-sectional profit variation is significantly lower than that within the periphery when the return on equity measure of profitability is used.

The same two risk measures were incorporated in this set of regression equations. The results with return on equity as the profit measure confirm those with the overall rate of return measure. The results show that risk as measured by the mean value of the TSD variable (temporal standard deviation of rate of return on equity) is significantly lower for the core group than for the periphery group for each of the slightly different core thresholds. Again, the results are consistent with the hypothesis that the expected tradeoff between temporal risk and return is reversed; core firms both earn higher rates of return and experience smaller temporal fluctuations in rate of return than do periphery firms.

The coefficients of the temporal risk variable are negative and significant for periphery firms in every year and negative and significant for core firms in every year except 1973, when the coefficient is positive and significant. The coefficient in the

TABLE 9

Cross-Sectional Variance of Profit Rates
(Return on Equity)

	(1) core sample variance	(2) periphery sample variance	(3) (2)/(1)
1969	.0049	.0311	6.35
1970	.0106	.1076	10.15
1971	.0086	.0712	8.28
1972	.0131	.1217	9.29
1973	.0026	.1571	60.42

core group is significantly more positive in three years while the coefficient in the periphery group is significantly more positive in one year and there is no significant difference in the remaining year (at the .01 level of significance).

The results on the risk–return relationship using leverage show that the mean level of leverage (the ratio of equity to assets) is lower for core firms than for periphery firms. (See Table 7.) Again there is in effect a negative intergroup relationship between the return on equity and leverage; the mean return is higher for core than for periphery firms while the leverage ratio is lower for core firms.

The relationship between return and leverage within core and periphery groups using the return on equity measure is consistent with that which exists using the overall rate of return measure. The coefficients of the leverage variable in the equations estimated for core and for periphery firms are positive and significant for both groups in every year, with the exception of 1973 for the periphery group when the coefficient is nonsignificant. As with the overall rate of return measure the coefficients for core and periphery groups are generally close in value.

Again these results are consistent with the hypothesis of chapter five that there is a different profit–risk tradeoff for core than for periphery firms, in the sense that core firms earn higher rates of return for a given level of risk, and consistent with the business-risk hypothesis within both groups.

The coefficients of the size variable exhibit a similar pattern to that in the earlier equations and the same caveats and conclusions apply here. The coefficients of the growth variables for both core and periphery show the largest discrepancy from the earlier results. While the coefficients on both the industry growth variable and the firm–industry growth differential variable were basically positive in the earlier regressions, they are basically nonsignificant in this set of regressions.

Finally, the industry capital–output ratio has a significant negative effect on core firm profit rates in every year while it has no significant effect on periphery firm profit rates in any year. This is the same pattern found in the first set of regressions.

SUMMARY

The results of the empirical tests provide support for the existence of size and concentration thresholds which define core and periphery firms.[24] Further, the empirical results support the hypothesis that core firms earn systematically higher profit rates than do periphery firms and that core firm profit rates show significantly less intragroup variation than do periphery firm profit rates.

The hypotheses about temporal risk are also supported by the statistical results. Core firms' profit rates vary significantly less over time than do the profit rates of periphery firms. The quality of core firm profit rates, measured by the joint attributes of mean profit rate and level of temporal risk, is significantly higher than that of periphery firms.

The hypotheses about financial risk are also supported by the empirical results. There is, in effect, a negative intergroup leverage–rate of return relation consistent with the hypothesis that core firms combine lower exposure to business risk with higher rates of return. In addition, within core and periphery groups there is a positive leverage–rate of return relation consistent with the business-risk hypothesis.

The results for the remaining independent variables are also consistent with the general core–periphery theory. Core firms tend to dominate industries which grow significantly more rapidly than other industries. Core firms' growth rates also tend to be closer to their industry growth rates than do periphery firm growth rates. Mean levels of the capital–output ratio tend to be higher in core-dominated industries, consistent with the existence of capital barriers to entry.

[24] See chapter seven for further discussion of the significance of the empirical results reported here.

The results, using an overall rate of return measure, are strongly supported when the analysis is repeated with a return on equity measure of profitability, despite the fact that such a measure is not considered appropriate for a test of the core–periphery hypothesis.

Conclusion

THIS study has delineated and provided empirical support for a theory of competition and the industrial structure based on the concepts of core and periphery. The historical evidence, the long-term IRS data, and the empirical analysis of the data set of this study provide, with increasing precision and statistical power, a consistent view of the role and performance of core and periphery firms. Core firms are large relative to all firms in the economy, possess significant market share held jointly with other core firms in one or more industries, and as a result earn profit rates which are significantly higher and less risky than those earned by periphery firms.

A review of the historical evidence suggests that core firms, formed in the merger movement at the turn of the century, had largely consolidated their market power by the latter half of the second decade of this century. These firms subsequently turned to diversification as a strategy in the late 1920s and the available historical information is consistent with the core–periphery view of the reasons underlying that diversification. It was almost exclusively very large firms which diversified and these firms were located primarily in relatively concentrated industries. These firms tended to diversify into industries which were closely related to their basic areas of expertise and which were technologically advanced and experiencing rapid growth. Further, these firms frequently diversified into industries where other similar firms held market positions. Such diversification efforts frequently resulted in positions of significant market power in the entered industry. Thus a picture emerges of core firms diversifying away from inadequate profit opportunities in their home industries into rapidly growing new industries where they frequently engaged in direct competition with other core firms.

One result of the expansion of core firms was a substantial increase in the level of aggregate concentration in manufacturing, interrupted by the period of the depression through World War II and apparently interrupted again by the economic upheavals of the 1970s. Evidence on the stability of core membership indicates that once a firm joins the ranks of the largest firms in the economy, a group which is roughly synonymous although not identical with the core, the probability of failure or even decline is almost negligible.

The historical evidence is consistent with the view that after the formation of the original core firms and the consolidation of their market positions, core firms maintained their dominant home industry positions, engaged in interindustry competition via diversification, and established positions of market power in the newly entered industries. The historical evidence also supports the view that core firms have increased their aggregate dominance over the economy since the early part of this century and that core firms once established seldom fail.

The basis for the bifurcation of the structure of competition is to be found in the turn-of-the-century merger movement, and the subsequent development of core and periphery firm competition cemented this divergence. The patterns of competition which emerged cut across industries, and interindustry competition was perhaps the most significant aspect of the new patterns of competition which emerged. Conceptions of competition linked primarily to individual industries are as a result not adequate to an analysis of large-firm competitive behavior. A conception of large firms with market power as static noncompetitive megatheres is also not adequate to such an analysis. The picture of core firms which emerges from the historical evidence is of dynamic, competitive firms aggressively engaged in interindustry efforts to extend their market power. The theory of core and periphery is thus an alternative to the traditional view of competition embodied in the industrial organization literature. In the core–periphery view, core firms' search for profitable new areas for investment of their relatively high profits results in diversification and frequent competition with other core firms as well as periphery firms. Core firm profit levels and behavior make potential competition a credible threat, which in turn reinforces the tendency toward equal core firm profit rates.

The traditional industrial organization view fails to take adequate account of interindustry capital flows. Related to that failure is the failure of the industrial organization literature to deal adequately with diversification as the large-scale phenomenon of the last fifty years which it has been for large firms. The view that potential competition or potential capital flows are significant and the view of beleagured oligopolies earning declining profit rates do not go well together. If typical oligopolies face competitive pressures which severely limit their profit rates, it is not clear where entrants or potential entrants to oligopoly or core-dominated industries come from. This view of inevitably declining dominant firms is also not consistent with the historical evidence that large firms face only a low probability of significant decline and exhibit remarkable longevity and stability.

The insistence, within the industrial organization literature, that "absolute size is absolutely irrelevant," also derives from a nearly exclusive focus on competition within industries. Although size and industry-specific market power are separable characteristics in theory, they are both required for core status, precisely because core firm competition frequently carries core firms outside their home industries into confrontations with other firms, where absolute size is an important contributor to success. While size relative to other firms in an industry is an important element of market power within the industry, once the focus of analysis turns beyond the industry, absolute size serves the same function at the level of the economy as a whole as does relative size within a particular industry. Absolute size gives a firm an advantage relative to all other firms in the economy and in particular relative to other firms which may be direct competitors in a particular area outside its home industry. The realm of competition for a core firm includes much more than the narrow industry of which it is defined to be a member.

Core firms possess substantial market power yet also compete actively. At the same time, active core firm competition does not produce the usual welfare benefits normally associated with competition. While such competition does serve to regulate the profit rates earned by core firms, the result of core competition is seemingly permanently superior performance for core firms when compared with periphery firms. Core firms succeed in retaining disproportionately high levels of profit and disproportionately low levels of risk when compared with other firms.

The central core–periphery hypothesis is that core firms and periphery firms compete in effectively separate regimes and that the results of that competition differ significantly between these regimes. This does not mean that core and periphery firms necessarily in different industries or produce different products. Core and periphery firms frequently coexist within industries, but within industries as in the economy as a whole, core and periphery firms constitute groups with distinct patterns of behavior and performance. In other words, the competitive dynamic for core firms is itself isolated from the competitive dynamic for periphery firms.

The different nature of competition for core firms results, according to the core–periphery hypothesis, in core firm profit rates higher than those of periphery firms. The fourteen years of IRS data provide preliminary evidence that core firms earned significantly higher profit rates than did periphery firms over a substantial period. The empirical results of this study also show that core firms earned significantly higher profit rates than did periphery firms in each of the five years for which the firm-specific data was analyzed; core firm profit rates were higher by from 25 to 58 percent than those of periphery firms. Core and periphery competition, according to this hypothesis, results in core profits which are not only higher but less risky than periphery firm profit rates. The empirical results show that by the two measures of risk employed, temporal variability and leverage, core firm profit rates were less risky in each of the five years tested. Core firm profit rates fluctuated significantly less than did periphery firm profit rates and leverage, maintained as an offset to business risk, was significantly lower for core firms than for periphery firms. The profit rates earned by core firms were thus of superior quality, in the sense that they were higher and there was lower risk associated with them, and did not represent a point on a positively sloped risk–return continuum shared with periphery firms. Core firm profit rates were superior as a result of the two key attributes of core firms, large size relative to all firms in the economy and large market share held jointly with other core firms in particular industries.

The attempt within the industrial organization literature to associate higher firm profit rates with efficiency alone requires a theory, that of the homogeneous product industry, which misses a central part of core firm characteristics and behavior. While production by core firms via large investments is undoubtedly highly efficient, it is not the fact of production efficiency in individual plants that is central to the superior performance of core firms. A relatively small firm could own a plant of maximum efficiency in most major U.S. industries, relatively concentrated or not. Core firms produce a broad product line, are diversified across industries, compete via product differentiation, creation, and marketing, and maintain a competitive position which can be broadly challenged only with very large amounts of capital. Core firms are qualitatively different than periphery firms. While size is required for core membership, size is not a proxy for efficiency. Size creates access to a realm of large-scale investments required to compete across the range of tactics employed by core firms and thus is required for and creates an element of market power. Large size together with significant market share held jointly with other large firms in an industry or industries requiring such investment, is required for the market power associated with core firm status.

Competition, however structured, establishes a relation between risk and return. The core–periphery hypothesis is that two distinct risk–return relationships are formed within the two competitive sectors and that the relationship within the core competitive sector is superior to that established within the periphery sector. Core and periphery firms are not on the same risk–return continuum. A linear bivariate risk–return relationship with return as a function of risk can be characterized by location, that is, intercept, and by shape, that is, slope. The empirical results show, for the temporal risk measure, that both slope and intercept are significantly different for core than for periphery firms. Core firms earn higher, less risky profit rates; the risk–return curve has a larger intercept for the core firm group than for the periphery firm group. The slope of the risk–return relationship is significantly less negative for core than for periphery firms; for every unit increase in risk there is a smaller reduction in the rate of return for core than for periphery firms. Taken together these attributes of the separate risk–return curves mean that for every level of risk core firms earn a higher rate of return than do periphery firms.

Not only is the relationship between temporal risk and return negative over all core and periphery firms as expected (in the sense that core firms have higher profits and lower temporal risk), but the risk–return relationship within the core and periphery groups is also negative, which was not expected. Insofar as temporal standard deviation is a measure of risk it is expected that within homogeneous groups of firms that there would be a positive risk–return relationship. This negative relation is consistent with some earlier results reported in the literature but a satisfactory explanation awaits further research.

The empirical results show that the risk–return relationship using the leverage measure has a different location for core firms than for periphery firms; again the risk–return curve has a larger intercept for the core firm group than for the periphery firm group. The shape of the tradeoff within each group is not significantly different. There is the expected positive risk–return relationship between rate of return and leverage in each group. Again, when taken together these two attributes of the risk–return curves mean that for every level of risk as measured by leverage, core firms earn a higher rate of return than do periphery firms.

Thus, using both the leverage measure and the temporal measure core firms exhibit a distinct and superior risk–return relationship when compared to that of periphery firms.

The results here on the financial risk–return tradeoff show a positive return–leverage relation within the core and periphery groups separately, which is reversed overall by the ability of core firms to combine high returns with relatively low leverage. The positive return–leverage relation within core and periphery groups is consistent with the hypothesis that leverage, the ratio of equity to assets, and a direct measure of financial risk, is used by firms to offset business risk and is therefore positively associated with business risk or the overall risk of the firm. The effectively negative return–leverage relation between groups is consistent with the core–periphery view that core firms do not give up higher returns for their lower risk.

Lower leverage in isolation is associated with increased financial risk, so choosing less leverage does not reduce risk to the firm and cannot represent an alternative to higher returns. In the core–periphery view, a firm's choice of leverage is directly dependent on the business risk faced by the firm. Thus core firms would only lower their leverage if their business risk were lower. Their business risk is lower as a result of their competitive strategy, which produces substantial market power and relative insulation from business risk when compared to periphery firms. These results are not consistent with the view that there is an underlying negative return–leverage relationship that is reversed by firms with market power, which take some of their advantage as lower risk rather than even higher returns, the quiet-life hypothesis.

The quiet-life hypothesis takes market power as given and suggests that firms may choose to take the benefits of market power as either higher returns or lower risk. Given the empirical results of this study, if the negative relation between leverage and return across core and periphery groups were to be explained as core firms choosing lower risk rather than even higher returns, it would imply that core firms choose between levels of market power. In order to explain the results of this study it would have to be argued that core firms choose lower business risk as an alternative to higher returns. Given that business risk is a negative function of market power and that return is a positive function of market power, this tradeoff is unlikely to exist. Rather, market power should simultaneously increase the rate of return and reduce business risk. Thus the results of this study suggest that core firms are not in search of the quiet life; core firms are profit maximizers. Core firms are the beneficiaries of a favorable confluence; the forms of core firm competition in the context of corespective behavior create the stable environment required for long-run profit maximization as well as high rates of return.

Finally, the core–periphery hypothesis is that as a result of the nature of core and periphery competition, there will be less cross-sectional profit rate variability among core firms than among periphery firms. This is the final element which distinguishes performance in the two competitive regimes. Core firms' market power and corespective behavior in their home industries together with core firm potential entry-related limit pricing and interindustry capital flows produce, in the core–periphery hypothesis, a tendency toward a more homogeneous rate of return among core than among periphery firms. The periphery firm competitive sector, by contrast, is characterized by a relative lack of interindustry competition and intraindustry competition constrained by exit barriers, intraperiphery mobility barriers, and higher temporal firm profit rate fluctuations than the core sector. The empirical results of this study show that there is significantly less cross-sectional profit rate variability among core firms than among periphery firms in each of the five years tested.

The empirical results of this study support other aspects of the core–periphery hypothesis, which were also confirmed by the historical evidence. Core-dominated industries were characterized by higher capital output ratios than the industries of periphery firms, consistent with capital barriers to entry. Core-dominated industries grew more rapidly than other industries. The firm–industry growth differential was smaller and showed less variation for core than periphery firms, consistent with the hypothesis that core firms within an industry tend to be more homogeneous than periphery firms within an industry.

Neither the statement of the core–periphery theory nor the empirical tests of that theory in this study take explicit account of international competition, whether that be a result of foreign-based companies competing in U.S. markets, U.S.-based companies competing in foreign markets, or U.S.-based companies producing abroad and importing to U.S. markets. If the core–periphery hypothesis is construed to be about competition within the U.S. economy and more precisely about the relative results of that competition for the core and periphery groups of firms, then the presence or absence of foreign competition does not affect the significance of tests of that hypothesis. If core firms significantly outperform periphery firms on a systematic basis, that fact is of central importance to an understanding of competition in the U.S. economy without regard to foreign competition.

The empirical results of this study account for import competition explicitly via adjustments to the concentration ratios and implicitly in that profit performance is by definition net of all competitive effects, whatever the source. The fact that significant profit rate and risk differentials existed for the years analyzed in this study suggests that foreign competition was not adequate to offset core firm advantages. From the core–periphery perspective, for increased foreign competition to be of significance it would have to produce a secular decline in the profit rate and risk differential between core and periphery firms on both an intra- and an interindustry basis. This study analyzes data from a period prior to the height of import competition in many U.S. markets. Analysis of the impact of such competition during the 1970s and an assessment of the trend in core–periphery differentials requires additional and more current data.

In the competition–monopoly view, the new foreign competition is seen as inconsistent with "monopoly" positions in domestic industries and likely to result in a restructuring of the affected industries on a more competitive, in the normative sense, basis. The core–periphery view is that intracore competition is expected, represents the usual pattern of competition and is consistent with ongoing core-firm domination of particular industries, albeit with the possible addition of several new core members, and therefore superior profit performance.

Although recent incursions by foreign producers represent a significant change in the intensity of competition in some industries, such competition does not by itself suggest that the market power of core firms must diminish. New competition from outside core firms may well result in the restructuring of dominant firm relationships within an industry. However, such restructuring does not imply that a qualitatively different relationship will result between the surviving core firms or between such core firms and periphery firms.

Current elevated levels of foreign competition do represent a real change in the character of competition within the U.S. and may result in the demise of some core firms. Even if increased competition for a particular industry results, in the extreme case, in the effective disappearance of a domestic industry and both the core and periphery firms which produced there, it would not necessarily be the case that competition was increased in a normative sense. This may represent one stage in the internationalization of core and periphery in which large foreign-based firms can underprice domestic producers for various reasons but still earn a relatively high profit rate and have the ability to raise prices subsequently.

While core firms have exhibited remarkable performance over the first three quarters of this century in terms of profitability, stability, growth, and longevity, there is no guarantee that core firms will continue to hold their place in the economy either individually or as a group. It is expected that the evolution of a more integrated world economy will produce an evolution of the world industrial structure similar to the development of core and periphery within the U.S.; not all core firms may make the transition successfully. The development of new technologies will pose formidable challenges to core firms both in producing and applying them. The ultimate outcome for particular core firms will be determined by their competitive response to foreign incursions and to technological change. Nonetheless, core firms are in a significantly better position to successfully meet such new challenges and competition than are periphery firms.

Bibliography

Adelman, M. A. 1951 "The Measurement of Industrial Concentration." *Review of Economics and Statistics* 33 (November):285–90.

———. 1965. Testimony in *Economic Concentration*, pt. 1. U.S. Congress, Senate, Subcommittee on Antitrust and Monopoly. Washington, D.C.: Government Printing Office.

Alexander, Sidney. 1949. "The Effect of Size of Manufacturing Corporation on the Distribution of the Rate of Return." *Review of Economics and Statistics* 31:229–35.

Allen, Bruce T. 1976. "Average Concentration in Manufacturing, 1947–1972." *Journal of Economic Issues* 10 (September):664–73.

Asch, Peter, and Matihayu Marcus. 1970. "Returns to Scale on Advertising." *Anti-Trust Bulletin* (Spring):33–41.

Averitt, Robert T. 1968. *The Dual Economy.* New York; W. W. Norton.

Bain, Joe. 1951. "Industrial Concentration and Antitrust Policy." In *The Growth of the American Economy*, ed. Harold F. Williamson. Englewood Cliffs, N.J.: Prentice-Hall.

———. 1956. *Barriers to New Competition.* Cambridge, Mass.: Harvard University Press.

———. 1968. *Industrial Organization.* 2nd ed. New York: Wiley.

Baker, Samuel H. 1973. "Risk, Leverage, and Profitability: An Industry Analysis." *Review of Economics and Statistics* 55 (November):503–507.

Baran, Paul, and Paul Sweezy. 1966. *Monopoly Capital.* New York: Monthly Review Press.

Bator, Francis, 1957. "The Simple Analytics of Welfare Maximization." *American Economic Review* 47 (March):22–59.

Baumol, William. 1967. *Business Behavior, Value, and Growth.* rev. ed. New York: Harcourt Brace and World.

———. 1982. "Contestable Markets: An Uprising in the Theory of

Industry Structure." *American Economic Review* 72 (March):1–15.

Berle, Adolph, and Gardiner Means. 1932. *The Modern Corporation and Private Property*. New York: Macmillan.

Berry, Charles. 1975. *Corporate Growth and Diversification*. Princeton: Princeton University Press.

Blair, John. 1972. *Economic Concentration*. New York: Harcourt Brace Jovanovich.

Bluestone, Barry. 1970. "The Tripartite Economy: Labor Markets and the Working Poor." *Poverty and Human Resources* 5 (July-August):15–35.

Bond, Ronald S. 1975. "Mergers and Mobility among the Largest Manufacturing Corporations, 1948 to 1968." *Antitrust Bulletin* 20 (Fall):505–19.

Boyle, Stanley, and Joseph McKenna. 1970. "The Mobility of the 100 and 200 Largest U.S. Manufacturing Corporations: 1919–1964." *Antitrust Bulletin* 15 (Fall):505–19.

Branch, Ben, and Bradley Gale. 1979. "Concentration versus Market Share: Which Determines Performance and Why Does It Matter?" Strategic Planning Institute. Typescript.

Brigham, Eugene. 1977. *Financial Management*. Hinsdale, Ill.: Dryden.

Brozen, Yale. 1971. "Bain's Concentration and Rates of Return Revisited." *Journal of Law and Economics* 14 (October):351–69.

Buchele, Robert. 1976. "Jobs and Workers: A Labor Market Segmentation Perspective on the Work Experience of Middle-Aged Men." Smith College. Typescript.

Burch, Philip. 1972. *The Managerial Revolution Reassessed*. Lexington, Mass.: D.C. Heath.

Cain, Glen. 1976. "The Challenge of Segmented Labor Market Theories to Orthodox Theory: A Survey." *Journal of Economics and Literature* 14 (December):1215–57.

Carleton, Willard T., and Irwin Silberman. 1977. "Joint Determination of Rate of Return and Capital Structure: An Econometric Analysis." *Journal of Finance* 32 (June):811-21.

Caves, Richard. 1970. "Uncertainty, Market Structure, and Performance: Galbraith as Conventional Wisdom." In *Industrial Organization and Economic Development*, ed. Jesse Markham and Gustav Papanek. Boston: Houghton Mifflin.

———. 1972. *American Industry: Structure, Conduct, Performance.* Englewood Cliffs, N.J.: Prentice-Hall.

———, B. T. Gale, and Michael Porter. 1977. "Interfirm Profitability Differences: Comment." *Quarterly Journal of Economics* 91 (November):667–80.

———, and Michael Porter. 1976. "Barriers to Exit." In *Essays in Industrial Organization in Honor of Joe S. Bain,* ed. R. T. Masson and P. T. Qualls. Cambridge, Mass.: Ballinger.

———, and Michael Porter. 1977. "From Entry Barriers to Mobility Barriers." *Quarterly Journal of Economics* 91 (May):241–61.

———, and B. S. Yamey. 1971. "Risk and Corporate Rate of Return: Comment." *Quarterly Journal of Economics* 85 (August) 513–17.

Chamberlin, E. H. 1933. *The Theory of Monopolistic Competition.* Cambridge: Harvard University Press.

Chandler, Alfred. 1959. "The Beginnings of 'Big Business' in American Industry." *Business History Review* 33 (Spring):1–31.

———. 1969. "The Structure of American Industry in the Twentieth Century." *Business History Review* 43 (Autumn):293–98.

———. 1977. *The Visible Hand.* Cambridge, Mass.: Harvard University Press.

Chow, G. 1960. "Tests of the Equality between Two Sets of Coefficients in Two Linear Regressions." *Econometrica* 28:561–605.

Clark, J. M. 1940. "Towards a Concept of Workable Competition." *American Economic Review* 30 (June):241–56.

Clark, Victor. 1929. *History of Manufacturers in the United States.* Vol. 2, *1860–1893.* New York: Peter Smith.

Clemens, Eli W. 1951. "Price Discrimination and the Multiple-Product Firm." *Review of Economic Studies* 19 (March):1–11.

Clifton, James, 1975. "Competitive Conditions in Theories of Price and Value." Ph.D. diss., University of Wisconsin.

Cochran, Thomas, and William Miller. 1961. *The Age of Enterprise.* rev. ed. New York: Harper.

Collins, Norman, and Lee Preston. 1961. "The Size Structure of the Largest Industrial Firms, 1909–1958." *American Economic Review* 51 (December):986–1011.

———. 1969. "Price-Cost Margins and Industry Structure." *Review of Economics and Statistics* 51 (August):271–86.

Cootner, Paul, and Daniel Holland. 1970. "Rate of Return and Business Risk." *Bell Journal of Economics* (Autumn):211–26.

Conrad, Gordon, and Irving Plotkin. 1968. "Risk-Return: U.S. Industry Pattern." *Harvard Business Review* (March-April):90–99.

Crum, William. 1939. *Corporate Size and Earning Power.* Cambridge, Mass.: Harvard University Press.

Cyert, R. M., and J. G. March. 1963. *A Behavioral Theory of the Firm.* Englewood Cliffs, N.J.: Prentice-Hall.

Demsetz, Harold. 1973a. "Industry Structure, Market Rivalry, and Public Policy." *Journal of Law and Economics* 161 (April):1–10.

———. 1973b. *The Market Concentration Doctrine.* Washington, D.C.: American Enterprise Institute.

Doeringer, Peter B., and Michael J. Piore. 1971. *Internal Labor Markets and Manpower Analysis.* Lexington, Mass: Lexington Books.

Edwards, Corwin. 1949. *Maintaining Competition.* New York: McGraw-Hill.

Edwards, Richard. 1975. "Stages in Corporate Stability and the Risks of Corporate Failure." *Journal of Economic History* 35 (June):428–57.

———. 1979. *Contested Terrain.* New York: Basic Books.

———, Michael Reich, and David Gordon, eds. 1975. *Labor Market Segmentation.* Lexington, Mass. Lexington Books.

Eichner, Alfred S. 1976. *The Megacorp and Oligopoly.* White Plains, N.Y.: M. E. Sharpe.

Elliot, J. W. 1972. "Control, Size, Growth, and Financial Performance in the Firm." *Journal of Financial and Quantitative Analysis* 7 (January):1309–20.

Ferguson, C. E. 1969. *Microeconomic Theory.* rev. ed. Homewood, Ill.: Richard D. Irwin.

Fisher, Franklin M. 1984. "The Misuse of Accounting Rates of Return: Reply." *American Economic Review* 74 (June):509–17.

———, and John J. McGowan. 1983. "On the Misuse of Accounting Rates of Return to Infer Monopoly Profits." *American Economic Review* 73 (March):82–97.

Fisher, I. N., and G. R. Hall. 1969. "Risk and Corporate Rate of Return." *Quarterly Journal of Economics* 85 (February):518–22.

Friedland, Seymour. 1957. "Turnover and Growth of the 50 Largest Industrial Firms, 1906–1950." *Review of Economics and Statistics* 39 (February):79–83.

Galbraith, John Kenneth. 1967. *The New Industrial State*. Boston: Houghton Mifflin.

———. 1973. *Economics and the Public Purpose*. Boston: Houghton Mifflin.

Gale, Bradley. 1972. "Market Share and Rate of Return." *Review of Economics and Statistics* 54 (November):412–55.

Gaskins, Darius W. 1971. "Dynamic Limit Pricing: Optimal Pricing Under Threat of Entry." *Journal of Economic Theory* 3 (September):306–22.

Goldschmid, H. J., H. M. Mann, and J. F. Weston, eds. 1974. *Industrial Concentration: The New Learning*. Boston: Little, Brown.

Gordon, David M., Richard Edwards, and Michael Reich. 1982. *Segmented Work, Divided Workers*. Cambridge: Cambridge University Press.

Gort, Michael. 1962. *Diversification and Integration in American Industry*. Princeton: Princeton University Press.

Hall, Marshall, and Leonard Weiss. 1967. "Firm Size and Profitability." *Review of Economics and Statistics* (August):319–31.

Herman, Edward. 1981. *Corporate Control, Corporate Power*. Cambridge: Cambridge University Press.

Hicks, J. R. 1935. "Annual Survey of Economic Theory: The Theory of Monopoly." *Econometrica* 3 (January):8.

Horowitz, Ira. 1984. "The Misuse of Accounting Rates of Return: Comment." *American Economic Review* 74 (June):492–93.

Hurdle, Gloria J. 1974. "Leverage, Risk, Market Structure, and Profitability." *Review of Economics and Statistics* 56 (November):481–82.

Intriligator, Michael et al. 1973. "Conceptual Framework of an Econometric Model of Industrial Organization." In *The Impact of Large Firms on the U.S. Economy*, ed. J. Fred Weston and Stanley Ornstein. Lexington, Mass.: Lexington Books.

Jensen, Michael, and William Meckling. 1976. "Theory of the Firm: Managerial Behavior, Agency Costs, and Ownership Structure." *Journal of Financial Economics* 3 (September):305–60.

Kaplan, A.D.H. 1954. *Big Enterprise in a Competitive System*. Washington, D.C.: Brookings Institution.

Kaysen, Carl, and Donald F. Turner. 1959. *Antitrust Policy*. Cambridge, Mass: Harvard University Press.

Kirkland, Edward. 1961. *Industry Comes of Age*. New York: Holt, Rinehart and Winston.

Kmenta, Jan. 1971. *Elements of Econometrics*. New York: Macmillan.

Kolko, Gabriel. 1963. *The Triumph of Conservatism*. Chicago: Quadrangle Books.

Kwoka, John. 1979. "The Effect of Market Share Distribution on Industry Performance." *Review of Economics and Statistics* 61 (February):101–109.

Larner, Robert. 1970. *Management Control and the Large Corporation*. Cambridge, Mass.: Dinellen.

Leibenstein, Harvey. 1966. "Allocative Efficiency vs. 'X-Efficiency.' " *American Economic Review* 56 (June):392–415.

Letwin, William. 1965. *Law and Economic Policy in America: The Evolution of the Sherman Act*. New York: Random House.

Livermore, Shaw. 1935. "The Success of Industrial Mergers." *Quarterly Journal of Economics* 49 (November):68–96.

Livesay, Harold, and Patrick Porter. 1969. "Vertical Integration in American Manufacturing, 1898–1948." *Journal of Economic History* 29 (September):494–500.

Long, William, and David Ravenscraft. 1984. "The Misuse of Accounting Rates of Return: Comment." *American Economic Review* 74 (June):494–500.

McConnell, Joseph. 1945. "Corporate Earnings by Size of Firm." *Survey of Current Business* 25 (May):6–12.

Mann, Michael. 1966. "Seller Concentration, Barriers to Entry, and Rates of Return in Thirty Industries." *Review of Economics and Statistics* 48 (August):296–307.

Manne, Henry. 1965. "Mergers and the Market for Corporate Control." *Journal of Political Economy* 73 (April):110–20.

Markham, Jesse. 1950. "An Alternative Approach to the Concept of Workable Competition." *American Economic Review* 40 (June):349–61.

———. 1965. "The Present War on Bigness: II." In *The Impact of Anti-Trust on Economic Growth*. New York: National Industrial Conference Board.

Marris, Robin. 1964. *The Economic Theory of Managerial Capitalism*. New York: Basic Books.

———, and Adrian Wood, eds. 1971. *The Corporate Economy*. Cambridge, Mass.: Harvard University Press.

Marshall, Alfred. 1970. *Industry and Trade*. 4th ed. New York: A. M. Kelley.

Mason, E. S. 1957. *Economic Concentration and the Monopoly Problem*. Cambridge, Mass.: Harvard University Press.

Means, Gardiner. 1965. Testimony in *Economic Concentration*, pt. 1. U.S. Congress, Senate, Subcommittee on Antitrust and Monopoly. Washington, D.C.: Government Printing Office.

Meehan, James W., and Thomas D. Duchesneau. 1973. "The Critical Level of Concentration: An Empirical Analysis." *Journal of Industrial Economics* 22 (September):21–36.

Melicher, Ronald W., David Rush, and Daryl Winn. 1976. "Industry Concentration, Financial Structure, and Profitability." *Financial Management* (Autumn):44–49.

Mermelstein, David. 1969. "Large Industrial Corporations and Asset Shares." *American Economic Review* 59 (September):531–41.

Modigliani, Franco. 1958. "New Developments on the Oligopoly Front." *Journal of Political Economy* 66 (June):215–32

Moody, John. 1904. *The Truth about the Trusts*. New York: Moody.

Mueller, Willard, and Larry Hamm. 1974. "Trends in Industrial Market Concentration, 1947-1970." *Review of Economics and Statistics* 56 (November):511–13.

Murphy, Kevin. 1985. "Corporate Performance and Managerial Remuneration." *Journal of Accounting and Economics*

Navin, Thomas. 1970. "The 500 Largest Industrials in 1917." *Business History Review* 44 (Autumn):360–86.

———, and Marion Sears. 1955. "The Rise of a Market for Industrial Securities." *Business History Review* (June):105–38.

Nelson, Ralph. 1959. *Merger Movements in American Industry: 1895-1956*. Princeton: Princeton University Press.

Neter, John, and William Wasserman. 1974. *Applied Linear Statistical Models*. Homewood, Ill.: Richard D. Irwin.

Newman, H. 1978. "Strategic Groups and the Structure-Performance Relationship." *Review of Economics and Statistics* (August):417–27.

Nutter, G. Warren, and Henry A. Einhorn. 1969. *Enterprise Monopoly in the United States, 1899–1958*. New York: Columbia University Press.

O'Connor, James. 1973. *The Fiscal Crisis of the State*. New York: St. Martins.

Ornstein, Stanley, 1972. "Concentration and Profits." *The Journal of Business* 45 (October):519–41.

Osborn, Richard. 1950. *Effects of Corporate Size on Efficiency and Profitability*. Urbana: University of Illinois Press.

———. 1970. "Concentration and the Profitability of Small Manufacturing Corporations." *Quarterly Review of Economics and Business* (Summer):15–26.

Oster, Gerry. 1978. "A Factor Analytic Test of the Dual Economy." *Review of Economics and Statistics* 61 (December):31–39.

Palmer, John. 1973. "The Profit-Performance Effects of the Separation of Ownership from Control in Large U.S. Industrial Corporations." *Bell Journal of Economics* 4 (Spring):293–303.

Penn, David. 1976. "Aggregate Concentration: A Statistical Note." *Antitrust Bulletin* (Spring):91–98.

Penrose, Edith. 1959. *The Theory of the Growth of the Firm*. New York: Wiley.

Porter, Michael E. 1976. *Interbrand Choice, Strategy and Bilateral Market Power*. Cambridge, Mass.: Harvard University Press.

Qualls, David. 1976. "Market Structure and Managerial Behavior." In *Essays on Industrial Organization in Honor of Joe S. Bain*, ed. Robert Masson and David Qualls. Cambridge, Mass.: Ballinger.

Radice, H. K. 1971. "Control Type, Profitability, and Growth in Large Firms." *Economic Journal* 81 (September):547–62.

Rhoades, S. A., and J. M. Cleaver. 1973. "The Nature of the Concentration-Price/Cost Margin Relationship for 352 Manufacturing Industries: 1967." *Southern Economic Journal* 40 (July):90–102.

Robinson, Joan. 1933. *The Economics of Imperfect Competition*. London: Macmillan.

Rumelt, Richard. 1974. *Strategy, Structure, and Economic Performance*. Boston: Graduate School of Business Administration, Harvard University.

Samuels, J. M., and D. J. Smyth. 1968. "Profits, Variability of Profits, and Firm Size." *Economica* (May):127–39.

Scherer, F. M. 1970. *Industrial Market Structure and Economic Performance*. Chicago: Rand McNally.

——— 1974. "Economies of Scale and Industrial Concentration." In *Industrial Concentration: The New Learning*, ed. H. J. Goldschmid, H. M. Mann, and J. F. Weston. Boston: Little, Brown.

———. 1980. *Industrial Market Structure and Economic Performance*. 2nd ed. Chicago: Rand McNally.

Schumpeter, Joseph. 1942. *Capitalism, Socialism, and Democracy.* New York: Harper.

Semmler, Willi. 1984. *Competition, Monopoly, and Differential Profit Rates.* New York: Columbia University Press.

Shepherd, William G. 1964. "Trends of Concentration in American Manufacturing Industries, 1947–1958." *Review of Economics and Statistics* 49 (May):200–212.

———. 1970. Market Power and Economic Welfare. New York: Random House.

———. 1972. "The Elements of Market Structure." *Review of Economics and Statistics* 54 (February):25–37.

———. 1979. *The Economics of Industrial Organization.* Englewood Cliffs, N.J.: Prentice-Hall.

———. 1982. "Causes of Increased Competition in the U.S. Economy, 1939–1980." *Review of Economics and Statistics* 64 (November):613–26.

———. 1984. "Contestability vs. Competition." *American Economic Review* 74 (September):572–86.

Sherman, Howard. 1968. *Profits in the United States.* Ithaca, N.Y. Cornell University Press.

Singh, Agit. 1971. *Take-Overs: Their Relevance to the Stock Market and the Theory of the Firm.* Cambridge: Cambridge University Press.

———. 1975. "Take-Overs, Economic Natural Selection, and the Theory of the Firm: Evidence from Postwar United Kingdom Experience." *Economic Journal* 85 (September):497–515.

Sosnick, Stephen. 1958. "A Critique of Concepts of Workable Competition." *Quarterly Journal of Economics* 72 (August):380–423.

Stauffer, Thomas. 1971a. "The Measurement of Corporate Rates of Return and the Marginal Efficiency of Capital." Ph.D. diss., Harvard University.

———. 1971b. "The Measurement of Corporate Rates of Return: A Generalized Formulation." *Bell Journal of Economics* 2 (Autumn):434–69.

Steindl, Josef. 1945. *Small and Big Business.* Oxford: Basil Blackwell.

———. 1952. *Maturity and Stagnation in American Capitalism.* Oxford: Basil Blackwell.

Stekler, H. O. 1963. *Profitability and Size of Firm.* Berkeley, University of California Press.

Stekler, H. O. 1964. "The Variability of Profitability with Size of Firm, 1947-1958." *Journal of the American Statistical Association* (December):1182–93.

Stigler, George. 1942. "Extent and Bases of Monopoly." *American Economic Review* 32 (June):1–22.

———. 1950. *Five Lectures on Economic Problems.* New York: Macmillan.

———. 1956. "The Statistics of Monopoly and Merger." *Journal of Political Economy* 64 (February):33–40.

———. 1957. "Perfect Competition, Historically Contemplated." *Journal of Political Economy* 65 (February):1–17.

———. 1963. *Capital and Rates of Return in Manufacturing Industries.* Princeton: Princeton University Press.

———. 1964. "A theory of oligopoly." *Journal of Political Economy* 72 (February):57–58.

———. 1968. *The Organization of Industry.* Homewood, Ill.: Irwin.

Stonebraker, Robert. 1976. "Corporate Profits and the Risk of Entry." *Review of Economics and Statistics* 58 (February):33–39.

Sullivan, Timothy. 1974. "Market Power, Profitability, and Financial Leverage." *Journal of Finance* 29 (December):1407–14.

———. 1978. "The Cost of Capital and the Market Power of Firms." *Review of Economics and Statistics* 60 (May):209–17.

———. 1982. "The Cost of Capital and the Market Power of Firms: Reply and Correction." *Review of Economics and Statistics* 64 (August):523–25.

Sweezy, Paul M. 1942. *The Theory of Capitalist Development.* New York: Monthly Review Press.

Sylos-Labini, Paolo. 1969. *Oligopoly and Technical Progress.* Rev. ed. Cambridge, Mass.: Harvard University Press.

Temin, Peter. 1964. *Iron and Steel in Nineteenth-Century America: An Economic Inquiry.* Cambridge, Mass.: Harvard University Press.

Thorelli, Hans. 1954. *Federal Antitrust Policy.* Baltimore: The Johns Hopkins University Press.

U.S. Bureau of the Census. 1965. *Historical Statistics of the United States: Colonial Times to 1957.* Washington, D.C.: Government Printing Office.

———. 1971. *Annual Survey of Manufactures.* Washington, D.C.: Government Printing Office.

———. various years. *Enterprise Statistics,* pt. 3: *Link of Census Es-*

tablishment and IRS Corporation Data. Washington, D.C.: Government Printing Office.

U.S. Congress. Senate. Subcommittee on Antitrust and Monopoly. 1964. *Hearings on Economic Concentration,* pt. 1. 88th Cong., 2nd sess. Washington, D.C.: Government Printing Office.

U.S. Federal Trade Commission. 1969. *Economic Report on Corporate Mergers.* Washington, D.C.: Government Printing Office.

———. 1979. *The Coal Industry.* Washington, D.C.: Government Printing Office.

———. 1980. *The Uranium Industry.* Washington, D.C.: Government Printing Office.

U.S. Internal Revenue Service. various years. *Source Book of Statistics of Income.* Washington, D.C.: Government Printing Office.

Van Breda, Michael. 1984. "The Misuse of Accounting Rates of Return: Comment." *American Economic Review* 74 (June):507–508.

Vatter, Harold. 1975. *The Drive to Industrial Maturity.* Westport, Conn.: Greenwood Press.

Weiss, Leonard. 1963. "Average Concentration Ratios and Industrial Performance." *Journal of Industrial Economics* (July):236–54.

———. 1971. "Quantitative studies of industrial organization." In *Frontiers of Quantitative Economics,* ed. Michael Intriligator. London: North-Holland.

———. 1972. "The Geographic Size of Markets in Manufacturing." *Review of Economics and Statistics* 54 (August):245–66.

———. 1974. "The Concentration–Profits Relationship and Antitrust." In *Industrial Concentration: The New Learning,* ed. H. J. Goldschmid, H. M. Mann, and J. F. Weston. Boston: Little, Brown.

Weston, J. Fred, and Stanley Ornstein, eds. 1973. *The Impact of Large Firms on the U.S. Economy.* Lexington, Mass.: Lexington Books.

White, Lawrence J. 1976. "Searching for the Critical Industrial Concentration Ratio." In *Studies in Non-Linear Estimation,* ed. S. Goldfeld and R. E. Quandt. Cambridge: Ballinger.

Wilcox, Clair. 1940. *Competition and Monopoly in American Industry.* Washington, D.C.: Government Printing Office.

Williamson, Harold, ed. 1951. *The Growth of the American Economy.* Englewood Cliffs, N.J.: Prentice-Hall.

Winn, Daryl. 1975. *Industrial Market Structure and Performance.* Ann Arbor: University of Michigan Press.

———. 1977. "On the Relations between Rates of Return, Risk, and Market Structure." *Quarterly Journal of Economics* 91 (February):157–63.

Worcester, Dean. 1957. "Why 'Dominant' Firms Decline." *Journal of Political Economy* 65 (August):338–47.

Index

monopoly, 71, 81, 99; and competition, 190
Mueller, Willard, 65

Navin, Thomas, 69
neoclassical economics, 3; competition in, 9, 12, 31, 38, 44, 154; and profit maximization, 14

O'Connor, James, 92
Ornstein, Stanley, 115
Osborn, Richard, 105, 117
Oster, Gerry, 93
ownership and control, 14; and the structure of management compensation, 15

periphery, 37; competition, 37; and core fire competition, 41; firms, definition of, 7; market niches, 39; mobility barriers, 38; profit rates, 38; sector, 28; segments, 28, 39
Porter, Michael E., 23n, 28n, 34n, 39n, 42n
potential competition, 84; and entry barriers, 87; and profit rates, 87
profit: and competition, 43; maximization, 12, 13, 14; reinvestment of, 32
profit rate: bifurcated, 9, 31; and concentration, 109, 151, 162; core firm, 9, 11, 35, 37, 167; cross-sectional variability of, 145, 170; and efficiency, 120, 125, 127; executive compensation and, 106; firm versus industry, 113; formation of, 8, 31, 33, 35, 43, 44, 154; heterogeneous, 9, 37, 38, 42, 87; homogeneous, 8, 34, 36, 87; and industry growth, 174; intraindustry dispersion, 149; and leverage, 140; limits on, 32; marginal, 35, 100; and market share,

122; measures of, 155, 174; periphery firm, 37, 43, 45, 167; post-entry, 35; and risk, 42, 44, 137, 152, 171; and size, 104, 173; and size–concentration interaction, 114, 120, 163

risk: aversion to, 13, 144; business, 134, 140, 173, 187; and concentration, 136; and cross-sectional profit variability, 146; financial, 134, 140, 172, 178, 187; and leverage, 139, 172, 178; and market power, 135; and profitability, 137, 171; and return, 10, 42, 44; temporal, 136, 152, 171, 177, 186
Rumelt, Richard, 55

Scherer, F. M., 27n, 88
Securities and Exchange Commission, 153
Shepherd, William G., 59, 71, 121, 124, 160
Sherman, Howard, 92, 105
size: and aggregate concentration, 76; and barriers to entry, 133; and concentration, 114, 120, 163; and core firms, 19; and cross-sectional profit variability, 146, 148; and efficiency, 132; and market power, 76; measure of, 160, 173; and profitability, 19, 104; relative, 125; threshold, 161
size effect, 114, 119; and risk, 139
Sosnick, Stephen, 82
Standard and Poor's, 153
Stauffer, Thomas, 155
Steindl, Josef, 92
Stekler, H. O., 136
Stigler, George, 24, 68, 76
Stonebraker, Robert, 149
strategic groups, 5
Sweezy, Paul, 35n, 92, 99

Library of Congress Cataloging-in-Publication Data

Bowring, Joseph.
Competition in a dual economy.

Bibliography: p.
Includes index.
1. Competition—Mathematical models. 2. Industrial
organization (Economic theory)—Mathematical models.
I. Title.
HD41.B687   1986   338.6'048'0724   85-43271
ISBN 0-691-04234-9 (alk. paper)

Joseph Bowring is an economist with the New Jersey
Board of Public Utilities.

GPSR Authorized Representative: Easy Access System Europe - Mustamäe tee
50, 10621 Tallinn, Estonia, gpsr.requests@easproject.com

www.ingramcontent.com/pod-product-compliance
Lightning Source LLC
Chambersburg PA
CBHW061212220326
41599CB00025B/4618